Anti-Oppressive Universal Design for Teachers

Anti-Oppressive Universal Design for Teachers: Building Equitable Classrooms provides a student-centered, culturally responsive blueprint for building sustainable and just educational practices. Marginalized students face complex educational barriers, and undoing educational injustice requires intentional practices designed to be explicitly anti-oppressive. Yet schools continue to adopt trendy "one size fits all" practices that benefit only some. This is not equity.

Author Diana Ma presents a framework that takes the principles of equity and humanizing pedagogy from anti-oppressive theories and the principles of multiplicity and flexible design from Universal Design for Learning (UDL). Together, these principles form a framework designed to dismantle specific systemic oppression. The Anti-Oppressive Universal Design framework is designed for educators who want to build practices that work for all students.

The book's flexible design tools will help teachers create anti-oppressive and equitable education that frees students to be their full authentic selves in the classroom. In addition, there are classroom strategies and stories to show how this model benefits both students and teachers, providing sustainable alternatives to prescriptive practices.

Diana Ma is an anti-oppressive educator and Chinese American author of Middle Grade and Young Adult books. She teaches at North Seattle College and has presented on Anti-Oppressive Universal Design as well as the importance of diverse representation at schools, libraries, and national conferences. Learn more about Diana on her website: Dianamaauthor.com

Equity and Social Justice in Education Series

Paul C. Gorski, Series Editor

Routledge's Equity and Social Justice in Education series is a publishing home for books that apply critical and transformative equity and social justice theories to the work of on-the-ground educators. Books in the series describe meaningful solutions to the racism, white supremacy, economic injustice, sexism, heterosexism, transphobia, ableism, neoliberalism, and other oppressive conditions that pervade schools and school districts.

Becoming an Everyday Changemaker
Healing and Justice at School
Alex Shevrin Venet

Embracing the Exceptions
Meeting the Needs of Neurodivergent Students of Color
JPB Gerald

Identity-Conscious Practice in Action
Shaping Equitable Schools and Classrooms
Liza Talusan

Social Studies for a Better World, Second Edition
An Anti-Oppressive Approach for Elementary Educators
Noreen Naseem Rodríguez and Katy Swalwell

Teaching Storytelling in Classrooms and Communities
Amplifying Student Voices and Inspiring Social Change
Maru Gonzalez, Michael Kokozos, and Christy Byrd

Igniting Real Change for Multilingual Learners
Equity and Advocacy in Action
Carly Spina

Anti-Oppressive Universal Design for Teachers
Building Equitable Classrooms
Diana Ma

Anti-Oppressive Universal Design for Teachers
Building Equitable Classrooms

Diana Ma

Routledge
Taylor & Francis Group
NEW YORK AND LONDON

Designed cover image: Getty Images

First published 2026
by Routledge
605 Third Avenue, New York, NY 10158

and by Routledge
4 Park Square, Milton Park, Abingdon, Oxon, OX14 4RN

Routledge is an imprint of the Taylor & Francis Group, an informa business

© 2026 Diana Ma

The right of Diana Ma to be identified as author of this work has been asserted in accordance with sections 77 and 78 of the Copyright, Designs and Patents Act 1988.

All rights reserved. No part of this book may be reprinted or reproduced or utilised in any form or by any electronic, mechanical, or other means, now known or hereafter invented, including photocopying and recording, or in any information storage or retrieval system, without permission in writing from the publishers.

Trademark notice: Product or corporate names may be trademarks or registered trademarks, and are used only for identification and explanation without intent to infringe.

ISBN: 978-1-032-76032-2 (pbk)
ISBN: 978-1-003-47680-1 (ebk)

DOI: 10.4324/9781003476801

Typeset in Palatino
by SPi Technologies India Pvt Ltd (Straive)

To my students, who have made teaching a true joy.

Contents

Preface viii
Acknowledgements xi
Meet the Author xiii

1 Why We Need Anti-Oppressive Universal Design 1

2 Designing Classrooms for Freedom 38

3 Building Equitable Curriculum and Practices
   with Anti-Oppressive Universal Design 67

4 Building Equitable Classroom Policies with
   Anti-Oppressive Universal Design 102

5 Reframing Accommodations with Anti-Oppressive
   Universal Design 131

6 Building Sustainable Teaching with Anti-Oppressive
   Universal Design 151

7 Building Equitable Assignments and Assessments
   with Anti-Oppressive Universal Design 171

Preface

If you're reading this book, you've probably already heard about Universal Design for Learning (UDL), a framework developed by the CAST organization (formerly Center for Applied Special Technology) to design accessible learning. Whenever the topic comes up, you might nod along but think to yourself, "Okay, I have some sense of UDL, but how do I actually use this framework in my classroom?" If so, you're not alone.

Initially, I had only the vaguest sense of what UDL actually was. I certainly didn't see the connection between UDL and the antiracist, social justice theories that I had worked hard to apply to my own teaching, but once I *did* see the connection between two ideologies that seek to create equitable access for students, I couldn't stop talking about it. I talked about the potential of an Anti-Oppressive Universal Design (UD) framework to other teachers, friends, students, colleagues, and anyone who would listen.

At some point, I stopped only talking about it and actually started to design classroom policies, curriculum, teaching practices, assignments, and assessments under an Anti-Oppressive UD framework. I knew this would have an effect—but I wasn't prepared for how much of an impact it had. Students reported feeling supported and empowered in their education, success rates skyrocketed, and (not incidentally) my teaching became infinitely more sustainable and joyous.

I wanted to write this book for educators who are interested in, or might even be familiar with UDL, and are curious to know why UDL needs an anti-oppressive foundation for truly equitable educational design. This book is also for educators who might already be seeped in anti-oppressive theories and are curious to know why we need a universal design lens to create even more equitable access for students.

My ultimate goal for this book is to explain what we, as teachers, can do to create positive learning and transformative possibilities for our students and ourselves. But before we can make these changes, we need to take a hard look at the policies and practices that many of us were trained in and that we, ourselves, might have been educated under. We must understand how our educational systems are failing students *and* teachers if we are going to make necessary changes.

Along those lines, I can promise you that this isn't one of those books that throw a bunch of depressing things at you without offering concrete strategies for change. I understand that this is the last thing you want, so I will try to make the payoff worth it. You have my word as a Young Adult (YA) romance author.

And, yes, you read that right.

Happily Ever After (or Happy For Now)

So, what does a YA romance novel have to do with a book about anti-oppressive education? It's simple. As an author of children's books, I'm aware that my readership want, need, and deserve books full of hope, and as an author of YA romance novels, I am a big believer in what is known in the business as Happily Ever After (HEA). Let me explain.

In a YA romance, the main characters are guaranteed an HEA at the end of the book. However, the journey to their HEA is full of challenges that spur growth and learning. The protagonists have to *earn* that HEA. Now, this doesn't mean that the HEA is going to be what the characters or readers might expect. It might not even be an HEA but rather an HFN (Happy For Now). But whatever it is, it has to be satisfying.

So that's what I'm going to do my best to deliver in this book—an HEA (or at least an HFN) that may require some overcoming of challenges and habits of thought but will ultimately be worth the effort because the best HEA is one that feels earned. Admittedly, the HEA in this case is going to take the form of skills and strategies developed under an Anti-Oppressive UD framework rather than a candlelit dinner and flowers, but the overall premise of a fulfilling, earned, and hopefully lasting HEA still holds true.

I'd also like to offer one more lesson I learned when I branched out from writing YA books and started writing Middle Grade books. What I learned is that in a Middle Grade book, the proportion of hope has to be greater than the difficulties. So, that's what I can promise you in this book—an HEA and a greater proportion of hope.

Along the way, I'll share my own stories and challenges and how I have had to grow and break free from my own assumptions and social conditioning. In other words, I'm not going to ask you to take this potentially difficult path without sharing the journey with you.

I have one last thing to say before we leave behind the topic of HEA, and if you are a reader of romances, then you already know this. Ultimately, it is not the HEA that makes the journey worth it. It is the journey itself that is worthwhile.

So, are you ready to embark on our journey to HEA/HFN with a large dose of hope? Great! Then let's begin.

Acknowledgements

Thank you to Paul Gorski, the editor of the fantastic *Equity and Social Justice in Education* series; Lauren Davis; and everyone at Routledge for being awesome and giving my book the perfect home!

There are many people who encouraged me to write this book about Anti-Oppressive Universal Design (UD), but I want to especially thank Christina Scheuer for coaching me so beautifully through this book and the care you took in helping me realize my vision. You are an amazing book coach, editor, and friend! Thank you also to Justina Rompogren and Dr. Nevien Shaabneh for reading early chapters and for your insightful feedback and wonderful support.

I also want to acknowledge two incredible teachers who have supported me and contributed to the writing of this book in countless ways. Thank you to Ananda Scott for generously taking the time and energy to talk over concepts in this book and always being a safe place for me to land. Thank you to Dr. Tanisha Brandon-Felder for sharing your knowledge and inspiring me with your vitally necessary work in educational equity and justice.

I have been fortunate to teach in a fantastic community of friends and colleagues, and I want to acknowledge a few of them here. Thank you to my co-teachers, whom I have learned so much from: Cathryn Cabral, Melissa Grinley, Karen Stuhldreher, Jane Harradine, and Ann Culligan. My colleagues Terri Chung and Laura McCracken have also been wonderful in their support of this book, as has my dean, Brian Palmer.

Thank you to We Need Diverse Books, The Highlights Foundation, the CAST organization, and North Seattle College. In addition, I want to thank my own teachers, especially Arlene Naganawa. And, of course, I want to thank my very earliest teachers: my parents Ching Shu Ma and Chao Chang Ma. Thank you to my brother David for being the first person I ever tried to teach. Thank you also to the following people for your encouragement: Joel Ozretich, Cam Kiliany, Alison Green Myers, and Autumn Allen.

No acknowledgement would be complete without expressing how grateful I am to my students who have shared their stories. This book is for you and made possible by you. Thank you also to my children. I hope you will tell your beautiful and powerful stories one day.

Finally, I want to thank all the teachers who are reading my book! What you do is so important, and I am grateful that you are willing to make space for Anti-Oppressive UD in your teaching.

Meet the Author

Diana Ma is a Chinese American author who writes Young Adult and Middle Grade books that feature kickass Asian American heroes. These were the kind of characters that, growing up as a Chinese American girl, she hungered to find in books. She believes that it's important for all kids to recognize themselves as the heroes of the books they read. Her belief that diverse books help us create a better world is what drives her writing. She has two wonderful kids of her own and wants them to grow up with books that represent them.

Diana teaches at North Seattle College and has presented on Anti-Oppressive Universal Design and the importance of diverse representation at schools, libraries, and national conferences. Diana was a 2019 We Need Diverse Books mentee with Swati Avashti. She was also a 2021–2023 Highlights Foundation Muslim Storytellers Fellow. Diana's debut novel *Heiress Apparently* was a 2021 Washington State Book Award finalist in the Young Adult Literature category. She is represented by Christa Heschke and Daniele Hunter of McIntosh and Otis.

Diana lives in a suburb of Seattle with her family. She loves romance, musicals, Jane Austen, fantasy, science fiction, superheroes, magic, monsters, and monster slayers—and she is always dreaming up new stories.

1

Why We Need Anti-Oppressive Universal Design

When I was three years old, my preschool offered parents a chance to have their children assessed to see if they were gifted. My mother volunteered me for this test, so a proctor pulled me from my play and sat me down at a table with a page from a coloring book and a simple direction: "Color inside the lines."

Thinking back to that experience, I have a *lot* of questions. Who designed the test? How was it decided that "giftedness" would be measured in this way? Why was the ability to follow directions so valued? Why were three-year-olds even being tested? It strikes me that this test perfectly illustrates the problem of how schools separate students by arbitrary measurements of ability and teach compliance and conformity.

It was, by the way, a test I failed.

I have absolutely no memory of this, but my mother reports that I looked her right in the eye, flashed her a mischievous smile… and proceeded to color everywhere *except* inside the lines. The tests that followed didn't go any better. "Draw a circle." I drew a square. Eventually, I grew bored and simply refused to do any more tests.

Needless to say, I wasn't assessed as gifted. In fact, my performance may have sparked some concern in the proctor, but my mother tells me she wasn't worried. She knew I *could* color within the lines, but I was having too much fun coloring wherever I wanted.

This story surprises me because I do not remember ever being that person. I have no memory of that much joy. When I tell friends this story, they're surprised too. As an adult, I'm not exactly known as a rule-breaker, but back then, I was unafraid and unselfconscious. That began to change the moment I started school.

In school, the lines I once gleefully ignored became the boundaries that defined normalcy, belonging, and safety. These were high stakes for me, a Chinese American girl from an immigrant family. Belonging and safety are not a given for BIPOC (Black, Indigenous, and People of Color) and other marginalized students. From an early age, we learn that we are supposed to earn belonging and safety by assimilating into white-centric, dominant norms. Maybe we were never directly told this, but we learned this message of assimilation from books, TV shows, playground dynamics, school structures, and everyday microaggressions.

For example, I used to bring delicious homemade lunches of spicy pickled cucumbers and flavorful marinated eggs to school. However, when kids held their noses and said, "Eww. That smells gross," I quickly learned that the food I ate wasn't considered "normal." Embarrassed by being different, I asked my mother to pack me bland sandwiches with thin rubbery American cheese slices instead of the food I loved.

In other words, the lines in school were ones I *had* to stay within, and if I couldn't, I assumed there was something wrong with me. Shame and self-doubt took the place of my earlier creativity and confidence. Sadly, this is what happens to many students. School's insistence on coloring inside the lines robs students of the joy and freedom to simply *be* who they are.

Now, I am both an educator and a mother of two BIPOC children. Though I have always used an anti-oppressive teaching framework, observing my children's experiences with educational injustice and forced assimilation started my journey toward creating an Anti-Oppressive Universal Design (UD) framework. I knew I could not design classes under the same systems that oppress my children.

As a parent *and* teacher committed to social justice, I had already incorporated antiracist and anticolonialist theories into my teaching and was committed to equitable and humanizing pedagogy. However, I knew there had to be an educational framework for school that not only addressed structural oppression but also could transform the rigid structures of compliance and conformity that restricted my children's learning and freedom to grow into their authentic selves.

This search led me to Universal Design for Learning (UDL), which is a framework for flexible educational design to make learning accessible for all students. UDL gave me a concrete way to talk to my children's teachers about flexible design in classroom curriculum and practices to support multiple means of learning. There might not be much that teachers can do about the standardized testing, learning outcomes, and district-mandated curriculums that restrict our students' learning and our own teaching, but I was starting to learn how UDL could help teachers design flexible and equitable classroom curriculum, practices, policies, assignments, and assessments to undo the harm of compliance and conformity.

Naturally, it was not long before I began to incorporate UDL principles into my own teaching. Once I did so, I saw how UDL and the anti-oppressive educational theories I had practiced for decades could be used together to design greater flexibility and equitable access for my own students. Eventually, I realized that I wanted to do more than simply use these two frameworks together. I wanted to merge anti-oppressive theories and UDL into an Anti-Oppressive UD framework that could guide me in designing flexible and equitable curriculum and practices—a framework that could free both my students and me from the injustice and rigidity of traditional education.

Anti-Oppressive UD is rooted in my beliefs that students cannot learn unless they have the freedom to be who they truly are and that none of us is free unless oppression is dismantled. The Anti-Oppressive UD framework breaks down the educational boundaries that keep students and teachers from becoming our fully authentic selves—*and* empowers us to build equitable education together.

Anti-Oppressive UD is more than the sum of its parts, but it will be useful to examine what those parts are and how they work together. My framework borrows from both UDL and anti-oppressive theories to create a new Anti-Oppressive UD framework, so this chapter will examine the foundation, principles, and purpose of:

- The UDL framework
- Anti-oppressive theories
- The Anti-Oppressive UD framework

What Is Universal Design for Learning?

UDL is a framework for flexible educational design developed by the CAST organization (formerly Center for Applied Special Technology) "to explore ways of using new technologies to provide better educational experiences to students with disabilities" (CAST, "Timeline of Innovation"). Since then, the organization has undergone many changes as it continues to evolve. CAST has moved away from the emphasis on special technology, and its focus is now "to help make learning inclusive and transformative for everyone" (CAST, "About Universal Design for Learning").

Before I discuss UDL any further, I want to acknowledge its foundation in the principles of Universal Design (UD). According to the Centre for Excellence in Universal Design, "Universal Design (UD) is the design and composition of an environment so that it can be accessed, understood and used to the greatest extent possible by all people regardless of their age, size, ability or disability" (CEUD, "About Universal Design"). CAST began to develop the UDL framework when UD as an inclusive concept was gaining traction in the architectural field and advocated for by the disabilities rights movement (CEUD, "History of Universal Design").

Basically, CAST took the principles of inclusive architectural design from UD and added the principles of brain development and education from the learning sciences to create UD for Learning. Instead of creating accessible buildings through architectural design structures such as wheelchair ramps and automatic doors that all people can use, UDL uses UD principles to create accessible *learning* through educational design structures that all students can use. The underlying premise of a UDL framework is that education should be flexibly designed to have *multiple means* so all students can learn. In fact, *multiple means* are the guiding principles of UDL. The three core UDL principles (CAST, "UDL Guidelines") are

- Multiple Means of Engagement
- Multiple Means of Representation
- Multiple Means of Action and Expression

Examples of using these multiple means for flexible educational design structures might be

- Multiple means of *engaging* students by connecting the curriculum to different student interests
- Multiple means of *representing* class content with differentiated headings in slide presentations
- Multiple Means for students to *act* on and *express* their learning through flexible design in assessment

According to the UDL Guidelines, these principles of multiple means are meant to help students *access* learning, *build* neural pathways, *internalize* learning, and reach the *goal* of becoming "expert learners" (CAST, "UDL Guidelines"). As you can see, the foundation of learning sciences strongly shapes the purpose of UDL to create "expert learners." Later, I'll address why the purpose of creating "expert learners" places undue emphasis on changing students, but first let's discuss how UDL addresses the restrictions of traditional education.

To explain how UDL counters the rigidity and "one size fits all" model of traditional education, I'd like to use a toy metaphor. I think of traditional education as being like that toy with the round holes and round pegs; all the little brightly colored pegs are exactly the same shape and size and fit into the holes perfectly. The toy also comes with a mallet we can use to pound the pegs into the holes, and all the pegs fit neatly into their pre-made slots.

But what happens if we try to pound a differently shaped peg—like a triangle or a square or a hexagon—into the round hole? Well, then it wouldn't fit no matter how hard we pounded on the peg, and the corners of the peg would get damaged and chipped and maybe even misshapen from being hammered in our efforts to fit it into the round hole. That's what traditional education does to students. It chips away at and damages students by trying to hammer them into the uniform slot that doesn't fit them.

UDL, on the other hand, replaces the mallet and round peg/round hole toy with a toy that has many differently shaped holes. These might be holes shaped like a diamond, circle, rectangle, square, oval, triangle, star, and hexagon. The best part is that there's no need to hammer the pieces into the toy, because there are many shaped holes to accommodate all the different shapes. That's how UDL accommodates students—by recognizing distinct structural inequities and providing multiple access points that fit each individual student. Instead of trying to change the peg to fit the toy, UDL changes the toy.

In other words, UDL emphasizes the need to move away from a "one size fits all" mindset and offers guidelines to design individualized, flexible, and multiple teaching methods, assignments, and assessments so all students can learn. The UDL framework emphasizes changing the classroom environment through *multiplicity* and *flexible design* rather than trying to change the student. In doing so, UDL counters the inequitable rigidity of traditional education.

That is why I use the UDL principles of multiple means of engagement, representation, and action and expression in the classroom. These are wonderfully useful and concrete tools. In fact, UDL could have made that preschool gifted evaluation test more accessible. For example, instead of giving me a random page out of a coloring book with the directions to "draw inside the lines," the proctor could have used *multiple means of engagement* to ask me what I was interested in (I'm pretty sure it was fairies, dragons, or unicorns) and then given me a dragon to color in. Instead of only giving me the verbal directions to "draw inside the lines," the proctor could have used multiple means of *representation* to show me a visual image of what they wanted me to do. When I refused to draw a rectangle, the proctor could have used *multiple means of action and expression* to demonstrate my understanding of the concept by drawing a rectangle and asking me what shape it was. The use of these three UDL principles of multiple means would have helped me *access* learning, *build* neural pathways, *internalize* learning, and reach the *goal* of becoming an expert learner.

If the proctor had used UDL principles to make the test more accessible, I might have been assessed as "gifted." Maybe I would have been included in a gifted program and benefited from the opportunities it afforded.

However, while UDL can provide greater inclusion, it does nothing to dismantle an inequitable system that segregates students on the basis of abilities. Instead of designing a more accessible test, we could simply stop testing three-year-olds for their supposed "giftedness" and do away with defacto segregated education. UDL is an important framework, but UDL, by itself, cannot undo the harms of structural inequities.

UDL, with its focus on how each student learns differently, is a wonderful tool for accessibility. We absolutely need the UDL principles of multiplicity and flexible design of classroom curriculum and practices. But that's not all we need. We need a framework focused on dismantling racist, ableist, and sexist structures, and we need to design education that empowers students to be their full authentic selves.

Moving Beyond the Learning Sciences of UDL

UDL is based in the learning sciences—how brains work. However, the kind of diversity we teach *to* and teach *from* needs to go beyond *just* neurodiversity. Yes, our brains are different, but we are more than our brains. To be truly equitable, we need to move beyond developing just the brain and empower our students to be their full authentic selves. We all come to education with diverse cultural identities and lived experiences. For us to bring our whole selves—body, brain, heart, and soul—into our education, we need more than principles based in learning sciences. We need our principles to include anti-oppressive theories that affirm *all* of who we are.

Practices informed by learning sciences might create *learning* access for students, but these practices do not necessarily address the ableism, racism, sexism, transphobia, heterosexism, and other forms of oppression that limit access. Any framework that seeks to address oppressive structural barriers will need principles drawn from antiracism, anticolonialism, feminism, disabilities justice, and other anti-oppressive theories. Not incidentally, this foundation of anti-oppressive theories will also create more expansive accessibility to learning that is at the heart of UDL.

That is why the purpose of the Anti-Oppressive UD framework is *not* to create "expert learners" or to build neural pathways. It is to use Anti-Oppressive UD principles, including *multiplicity* and *flexible design*, to dismantle oppressive and rigid structures and to build systems that support students to be more fully themselves in the classroom rather than systems that work to change them.

The purposes of Anti-Oppressive UD and the purposes of UDL are not mutually exclusive, but if we focus *only* on creating expert learners or building neural pathways, then our focus is still on changing students. Rather than helping students adapt to the existing system, we need to focus on challenging the overall structures that harm our students in order to create new, more equitable models.

To design truly equitable education for our students, we need an anti-oppressive framework that specifically addresses systemic injustice. We must first understand and resist the institutional racism, sexism, economic injustice, ableism, and heterosexism that create barriers for our students before we can dismantle those barriers and empower our students. We cannot undo the barriers we do not recognize, and we cannot build new structures until we recognize the inequities of the old structures.

To come back to the toy metaphor, it is not enough to replace one restrictive toy with another toy. The new toy might provide more access in the form of multiple differently shaped holes, but it does nothing to address the systemic inequities that shaped the holes or the toy itself in the first place. For that, our educational framework needs a solid foundation of anti-oppressive theories.

What Is Anti-Oppressive Education?

My own anti-oppression pedagogy is based on theories such as antiracism, anticolonialism, feminism, and disabilities justice. The goal of these anti-oppressive theories is to dismantle the systemic racism, colonialism, economic injustice, sexism, heterosexism, transphobia, and ableism in institutions like healthcare, government, law enforcement, media, and of course… education.

One example of educational oppression is that the school curriculum has been dominated by white-centric history and texts based on a Western canon. Many students have shared with me that this has been their experience, and it was certainly my experience going through school.

In a photo album belonging to my parents, there is a picture of me around age ten that reveals the subtle everyday effects of a white-centric canon. In this picture, I'm reading one of many children's books with a white main character. My hair is in large plastic curlers that I remember painfully pulling against my scalp. I was trying to turn my straight black hair into the sleek bouncy curls of the white girls I saw in books and on TV—but what I got instead was a mass of frizzy hair and split ends. Like the book I was reading, the curlers were not made for me.

I'm not saying that my lack of access to books about BIPOC girls made me want to be white. But I am saying that I needed to see my hair, culture, and identity represented in the books I read to understand that I did not have to change who I was.

I want to emphasize that a white-centric curriculum does immense harm. It creates the illusion of white superiority and devalues and erases the histories, stories, cultures, and voices of BIPOC students. When students do not see themselves represented in the school curriculum, they do not have access to full expression of their cultures and identities and begin to question their own worth.

In addition, the Western canon is not formed with value-neutral standards. It is a body of work based on conquest and erasure of non-white literature. These "standard" curriculums are really a white-centric curriculum that BIPOC students are forced to conform to.

Many educational traditions and standards are based on a foundation of oppression. A horrific example in the United States is Indian boarding schools in the nineteenth century. These schools were designed with the sole purpose of forcing kidnapped Native American students to conform to white standards and culture and to erase their own. In the words of Captain Richard H. Pratt, the founder of the infamous Carlisle Indian Industrial School, the mission of these schools was to "Kill the Indian, and save the man" ("In the White Man's Image"). Education here was used as a "primary tool of conquest" (Gunn Allen, "Introduction" to *Spider Woman's Granddaughters*).

It is heartbreaking that Pratt and other white founders of these boarding schools felt the culture and language of their Native American students were "deficits" to be fixed so they could become productive citizens of white society. To be clear, the function of these boarding schools was not to develop future leaders, inventors, or artists but to train compliant servants for white families. That is, these schools were designed with the express purpose of maintaining white supremacy and forcing compliance.

While today's schools are not as egregiously harmful in their practices or goals, the seeds of colonialism are still present in the conformity and deficit models of education. For example, many schools hold workshops on developing grit, growth mindset, back-to-basics learning, and study skills where teachers are trained in "interventions" to help students develop the behaviors and mindsets to be more successful in school.

You could think of traditional education as an oppressive machine that must be dismantled for the possibility of educational equity to be realized. This is due to the way the machine of traditional education works—it shapes students into uniform molds—forcing marginalized students to conform to white-centric curricula and other oppressive norms such as ableist expectations. In this metaphor, students are both the end product the machine attempts to create as well as the cogs that make the machine work. Teachers and administrators are also cogs that make the machine work. Cogs, which are the teeth on the edges of a gear, have a very passive function.

Technically, it's the gear that turns and not the cogs. The only function of a cog is to fit into another cog of another gear so that all the gears turn in a synchronous pattern. However, if the cog doesn't fit within the cog of an adjacent gear, then all the gears stop turning, and the machine stops working. That's why standardized learning outcomes, testing, and curriculums are so much a part of traditional education—these are all measures to make the cogs fit, grease the gears, and keep the machine working. As cogs, none of us is supposed to question our function of fitting within the other cogs or what kind of gears we are turning—the gears of systemic injustice.

I have to admit that I used to think some of the initiatives that kept the traditional education machine running were great. After all, I wanted to help my students be more successful, and that is exactly what these growth-mindset, grit, back-to-basics learning, and study skills initiatives promise. The workshops emphasize the goal of helping students be successful by changing students' behaviors and mindsets. They certainly do *not* say they want to "fix" student "deficits" or remove student differences in the name of conformity. If they had, I would have rejected these initiatives immediately.

Like most teachers, I do not think of my students as deficient, nor do I think of enforcing conformity as my goal. However, the machine does not take into account our individual beliefs and goals; it simply grinds on, mindlessly fulfilling its function to chip away differences as if they were deficits. These well-meaning initiatives come from the oppressive ideology that students need to be fixed in order to fit into the dominant society. In other words, they are meant to help students better fit the machine.

The implicit assumption is that students' lack of grit, persistence, basics, or study skills is keeping them from being successful. But innate deficits are *not* the problem—an unjust system is the problem. The Native American students of the Carlisle School did not need to be fixed through genocidal practices. They did not need to conform to white-centric norms and lose their culture and language. They did not need to be assimilated into white colonialist systems of dominance. It was the colonialist school system that needed to be fixed or, rather, to be dismantled. In other words, we have to turn our focus to fixing the injustice in our school structures rather than supposed deficits in our students.

To give another example, Jean Anyon, in her article "Social Class and the Hidden Curriculum of Work," examines how classroom curriculum and practices are based on the inequitable socioeconomic class structures of our larger society. For example, in the schools that Anyon categorized as "Working-class," students were being trained to follow directions in their work. They were also expected to follow strict classroom rules. On the other hand, the "Middle-class," "Affluent Professional," and "Executive Elite" schools focused respectively on right answers, creativity, and analytical thinking in their work. The students in these three types of schools also had more freedom in the classroom than those in the Working-class school. Anyon comes to the conclusion that classroom work is training students to meet the expectations of their presumed future professions, replicating existing class disparities.

The truth is that traditional education was founded on a history of colonialism, racism, economic injustice, ableism, and sexism, and it works just as it is designed—in that it is socially, historically, and politically constructed to reinforce power and privilege in the United States. The positive and hopeful part of this, however, is that we *can* transform this oppressive system.

The unjust structures of racism, colonialism, ableism, and economic injustice are embedded within our classroom policies, curriculum, practices, assignments, and assessments. It's *those* things we need to redesign—not our students themselves. Yes, we are confronting an inequitable system, but the answer is not to make better cogs or oil the gears. We cannot base our educational practices on a legacy of injustice, no matter how well meaning our present-day school initiatives are. We cannot fix the machine, nor can we replace it with a better machine. We have to tear down the machine.

And that is what anti-oppressive education does. It dismantles the machine.

The main goal of anti-oppressive education is to dismantle the systemic racism, colonialism, economic injustice, antisemitism, anti-Muslim hate, anti-immigrant hate, sexism, heterosexism, transphobia, and ableism in education. Anti-oppressive pedagogy is a framework that is built upon theories from

- Antiracism
- Anticolonialism/Postcolonialism
- Feminism
- Queer Studies
- Disability justice

Essentially, the anti-oppressive framework helps us recognize how different types of oppression operate and how to resist them. Oppression is an inequitable and dehumanizing machine that reduces us to cogs. That is why we need an anti-oppressive framework to understand how the machinery of racism, sexism, ableism, economic injustice, and colonialism perpetuates inequities, forces us to conform to historically unjust systems, and keeps us from being our fully humanized selves. Only then can we be free of the machine and be our authentic selves.

Why Anti-Oppressive Education Needs to Be Equity-Focused

Anti-oppressive education focuses on dismantling the oppressive system because including more people in an inequitable system would not result in educational justice. Anti-oppressive education is different from inclusive education, which focuses on including more students into an inequitable system without necessarily changing the system itself. The intent of inclusion is, no doubt, a positive one, but it will not be successful unless systemic injustice is also addressed. Anti-oppressive education is *equity-focused* for the purpose of *breaking down larger systemic injustice*. Anti-oppressive education is not *equality*-focused or *inclusion*-focused. Equity is not the same as equality, and anti-oppression is not the same as inclusion, although these terms are often mistakenly conflated.

Equity is the belief that we must recognize the specific and distinct barriers students face in order to design socially just education. Equity is focused on justice rather than fairness. Treating everyone fairly will not directly address racism, sexism, economic injustice, and ableism. Instead, we need to build systems that intentionally fight injustice. Equitable education is differentially designed to dismantle racism, sexism, economic injustice, and ableism in our structures, policies, practices, curriculum, assignments, and assessments. Equity-focused education values and affirms differences.

Equality, on the other hand, is the belief that we must treat everyone the same and provide the same rights and access to everyone. The goal of equality is fairness. The flaw in the equality model is that it misses how the oppression of racism, economic injustice, sexism, and ableism creates differentiated harm and disparity that cannot be undone simply by treating everyone fairly as if privilege and oppression do not exist. Equal education is based on consistent and standardized structures, policies, practices, curriculum, assignments, and assessments. Equality-focused education results in structures normed on students with privileged identities.

Anti-oppressive pedagogy requires us to critically examine the structures of power in order to undo inequity, and that means recognizing that while some people have certain privileges—such as white privilege, cisgender privilege, and nondisabled privilege—others experience oppression—such as racism, transphobia, and ableism. One myth is that teaching about the harm of oppression in our past and present will only stoke division. For example, those who want to ban critical race theory and DEI (diversity, equity, and inclusion) offices from schools argue that teaching about or even acknowledging differences would actually *create* inequity. However, teaching about privilege and oppression is not what creates division. Inequitable divides already exist in the world, and ignoring injustice will not make it go away. We cannot work toward equity and connection until we recognize how oppression divides us.

For example, a school that has gendered bathrooms marked "male" and "female" has inequity literally built into its structure. A cisgender student (whose gender identity conforms to the gender they were assigned at birth) has the cisgender privilege of using the bathroom that matches their gender identity with no one questioning their right to use it. However, a trans student (whose gender identity does not conform to the gender they were assigned at birth) will often be questioned or even forbidden from using a bathroom that matches their gender identity. A nonbinary student (their gender identity does not conform to the binary of male or female) would not even be able to find a bathroom that matches their identity. In other words, trans and nonbinary students experience oppression while cisgender students experience privilege. I knew one trans student who had to run to a nearby fast-food restaurant to use the bathroom because their school did not have any gender-neutral bathrooms.

Pretending this inequity does not exist will not make it go away. Stop-gap measures can help, but the structures themselves need to be dismantled to have true equity. Without addressing the structural inequity itself, the best case-scenario is for an understanding teacher or counselor to quietly take a trans or nonbinary student aside and privately give them access to a staff bathroom. This might solve the problem of access in the short term, but it does not create structural equity where the system is *designed* to be equitable. I do want to be clear that, of course, we should be meeting students' need for access at the moment, and that might mean providing a trans student access to a staff bathroom. We just need to understand that better access does nothing to address the transphobia that restricted the student's access in the first place.

That is why oppression has to be named and long-term measures for structural change need to be explicitly anti-oppressive. Otherwise, the measures taken will be seen as an individual problem to be solved. For example, other students might see a trans student's access to a staff bathroom as a "special" right or need rather than a human right and need. Another consequence is that the student might feel the stigma of being marked as different and "other." On the other hand, it would be entirely different if the school communicated that the measures they take are meant to address the structural problem of transphobic systems—not to solve an individual access problem. The result might then be an equitable structure that included gender-neutral bathrooms so students are free to be different without being othered.

Structural equity requires the acknowledgement that a system that marks bathrooms on the strict gender binary of "male" and "female" is inherently oppressive in that it grants cisgender students the automatic privilege of using the bathroom that matches their gender identity and denies trans and nonbinary students the same automatic privilege. We need to recognize oppressive systems in order to dismantle and replace them with equitable ones.

Unlike an equity mindset that acknowledges and seeks to dismantle systemic oppression, an equality mindset that assumes that all students should be taught in the same way will not work to remove distinct structural barriers. In fact, treating everyone *equally* would actually be *inequitable* and unjust because it would ignore the social, historical, and cultural privilege that white, cisgender, male, straight, middle- and upper-class, nondisabled students have. Our ultimate goal should not be to design a "one size fits all" education with "special" rights, services, and education tacked on to create *equal* access. Rather, we should be focused on *equity*—recognizing the distinct differences of race, gender, disabilities, and so on and breaking down the specific type of structural barriers that confront students. Equity cannot be achieved by creating a better machine. Equity can be achieved only by destroying the machinery that perpetuates injustice.

Why Anti-Oppressive Education Needs to Be Intersectional

Anti-oppressive pedagogy is intersectional—rooted in the belief that none of us can be free until *all* of us are free. I recognize that the struggles to end racism, colonialism, sexism, transphobia, ableism, and economic injustice are all connected and that undoing only one form of oppression is not enough. That is why anti-oppressive education needs to be intersectional. *Intersectionality* is the concept that a person's multiple socially constructed cultural identities intersect in ways that shape experiences of oppression and privilege—including educational experiences. Feminist and legal scholar Kimberlé Crenshaw coined the term intersectionality to describe the intersecting oppression of racism and sexism that Black women experience in the legal system.

Intersectionality is a concept that acknowledges the interrelated struggles for educational freedom. For example, an intersectional lens allows us to recognize that a disabled BIPOC student is not free from educational oppression unless systems of racism *and* ableism are dismantled. In their blog post "Disability Justice - a working draft" for *Sins Invalid*, activist Patty Berne describes intersectionality as "a primary principle of Disability Justice." Berne goes on to discuss Disabilities Justice as an intersectional framework created by disabled activists of color who recognize "that each person has multiple community identifications, and that each identity can be a site of privilege or oppression." This is also a framework that recognizes the "disability experience itself being shaped by race, gender, class, gender expression, historical moment, relationship to colonization and more" (Berne). The purpose of the disability justice framework is to dismantle not only systems of ableism but also other intertwined oppressive systems such as racism, heterosexism, and transphobia.

The intersectionality of disability justice is relevant to our discussion of educational freedom because we need to recognize that "single issue identity based" (Berne) educational structures, policies, and initiatives do not address the educational experiences shaped by multiple and intersectional identities that can be a "site of privilege and oppression." An intersectional lens is necessary to understand the specific systemic barriers that confront students with multiple, intersecting identities so that all students can be free to be themselves.

For example, in my earlier example of other kids making fun of my homemade lunches, the school might have addressed this as an issue of systemic racism and even made anti-oppressive systemic changes that resulted in a diverse curriculum that affirmed Chinese culture and food. However, to fully understand my experience, we would need to look at it through the lens of intersectionality and recognize my identity as a Chinese Muslim. In fact, the main reason my mother packed my lunches is that my parents worried that the school cafeteria did not serve enough non-pork options or make clear enough which menu items had pork in them.

If my school had addressed only systemic racism, they would have missed the need to address the systemic Islamophobia that also shaped my experience. Let's say the school saw the need to provide non-pork, halal, and kosher options for Muslim and Jewish students. This, like creating a more diverse curriculum, would be inclusive and necessary. However, we would not fully understand my experience as a Hui, Chinese Muslim girl until we examine the intersections of race and religious cultural identity. Only then would we see how I had already been marked as different and other as Chinese in a system that valued conformity. How was I to fully embrace my own identity as a Chinese Muslim when being Muslim was also marked as being "other"? The answer would lie in systemic changes that recognize and affirm multiple, intersecting identities.

The school curriculum, for example, could have been expanded to include Chinese American stories as well as Muslim American stories. However, it's doubtful that Chinese Muslim stories would have been included because my intersectional identity is largely invisible in the United States (which is why I wrote *Rainbow Fair*, my middle-grade book about a Chinese Muslim girl). I want to acknowledge that it is, of course, impossible to include all the multiple identities that our students have. But that is another reason to shift from a purely inclusive model and toward a model that creates student choice in shaping the curriculum and empowers students in expressing the fullness of their intersectional identities, which I will talk more about in Chapters 2 and 3.

My point here is that intersectionality is an important aspect of equity because it allows us to understand the specific ways that systems intersect to shape students' experiences so we can work to undo systemic injustice to affirm, represent, and humanize students in all their multiple, intersecting identities. In other words, affirmation and representation of intersectional identities are deeply humanizing pedagogical practices.

Anti-Oppressive Education Is Rooted in Humanizing Pedagogy

I believe that education should be humanizing and designed for liberation from oppressive educational systems. Therefore, my anti-oppressive pedagogy is rooted in liberatory pedagogy, sometimes called critical pedagogy. Liberatory pedagogy is the practice of freeing students and teachers from the dehumanization of oppressive power structures. Paulo Freire, Brazilian activist, scholar, and educator, is one of the main theorists of liberatory pedagogy. In his book *Pedagogy of the Oppressed*, Freire says a lot about oppression, much of it complex, but his core belief is fairly straightforward—oppression is dehumanization, and *humanizing pedagogy* frees us from oppression. An anti-oppressive educational framework needs to be grounded in this liberatory pedagogy so that humanizing curriculum and practices can free students from oppressive educational structures.

Although Freire based his theories in the anticolonialist class struggles of Latin America, other scholars have applied his ideas to analyze other systems of oppression, drawing the conclusion that systemic racism dehumanizes people of color, systemic sexism dehumanizes women and nonbinary and trans people, systemic ableism dehumanizes disabled people, and so on. For example, bell hooks, Black feminist author of *Teaching to Transgress: Education as the Practice of Freedom*, draws from Freire's ideas to argue that teaching should be "a practice of freedom" that can and must transgress the racist and sexist structures of education. Only then can students and teachers alike be liberated from systemic injustice. In other words, we need to destroy the machine to be free.

Although anti-oppressive theories like antiracism and anti-colonialism are rooted in the dismantling of oppressive systems, anti-oppressive pedagogy is not a destructive or nihilistic framework. On the contrary, it is a framework of creativity and freedom. The traditional education machine relies on every single cog staying in place and mindlessly doing its job, but we are not cogs. We can say, "Hey, I'm not a cog. I'm a human being, and I refuse to be a part of this machine." Perhaps it is not enough if only one of us tries to stop the machine, but an intentional community working together to build strategies for joy and freedom in our classrooms *can* stop the machine.

In other words, we might not have a say in the larger structures of traditional education, but we *can* design our classroom policies, curriculum, practices, assignments, and assessments to resist the dehumanizing oppression of the machine of traditional education.

Anti-Oppressive Education Is Necessary and Intuitive

Anti-oppressive education is necessary and humanizing because it is rooted in equity, and it is not inordinately difficult to teach. Yet I have heard some teachers express support for anti-oppressive education but say they are uncertain how they might teach in antiracist and other anti-oppressive ways in a math or science or art class.

I understand this line of thinking, but we need to keep in mind that in whatever discipline we teach, many of our students have experienced the harm of educational injustice. Some bring with them the internalized ideas that they're just not good at writing or math. Some are convinced that they are simply "bad students"—because that's what our deficit-model traditional educational system has taught them to believe. No matter what discipline we teach, we have a responsibility to try to undo that harm.

Fortunately, anti-oppressive education in the classroom is not as difficult as it might seem. One simple strategy is using diverse texts and examples in our teaching. For example, a science teacher could talk about contributions to science made by scientists of color, women, trans, nonbinary, neurodiverse scientists, and so on. Highlighting such diversity would not take an inordinate amount of effort, yet it can make a profound difference in our students' lives to see their identities positively and fully represented in their education. The more we expand our teaching to be anti-oppressive, the more it becomes intuitive and humanizing as well as an equitable practice.

So… if anti-oppressive education is necessary to resist injustice and isn't too difficult to practice in the classroom, then why don't we go ahead and break the machine of traditional education? Good question. One reason might be that inclusion and equality models have created a machine that is not quite as damaging to students. However, I still believe we need to take down the machine—some damage is still too much.

Another reason the traditional education is still in place might be that teachers are often told to uphold conformity and deficit-thinking. Of course, that is not how these values are presented. Instead, many of us are told to support our students, hold them to normed standards, treat them equally, and make sure our practices and policies are consistent—and we're told to do all this in the name of fairness. It's no surprise that some of us go along with this well-meaning model. After all, our profession is generally made up of people who want to help and do good in the world, and words like "support," "standards," "equality," and "consistency" sound like they're good things. However, any "one size fits all" model, no matter how well intentioned, is inherently restrictive.

Of course, some students *are* able to achieve the trappings of success through the conformist and deficit models like grit and back-to-basics, but this is problematic because it requires students to conform to the structures of traditional education to achieve success. Some are able to do so because their privilege removes the structural barriers inherent in the educational system. This was certainly true for me, a cisgender student who grew up in a middle-class family, in terms of cisgender and class privilege.

Other students achieve educational success by losing a part of themselves in profoundly aching ways. This was also true for me, a Muslim girl of color with immigrant parents. To understand what parts of myself I lost, I needed to examine my own educational experience. In doing this, I had to look at the ways in which oppression has created barriers in my educational journey as well as the ways that privilege has helped me navigate the educational system.

Once I did this examination, I realized that I had been stuck replicating the same oppressive practices that I had unquestioningly accepted because of my privilege and/or internalization of the oppression I experienced. It was painful but necessary to realize that I had based my teaching on flawed practices.

For too much of my teaching career, I commented extensively on essays to justify a grade, required many difficult readings and long assignments, taught highly structured note-taking and essay organization, required reading journals and vocabulary lists, and stressed the importance of regular, punctual attendance. I believed I was doing the right thing.

I believed that I would be lowering standards if I didn't require my students to work hard, learn the basics of writing, and abide by rigid attendance policies.

I believed that if I reduced the workload, encouraged multiple forms of written expressions, and offered flexible attendance, then I was expecting less of my students and depriving them of necessary skills they would need to be successful in school and in life.

After all, conforming to those expectations of school worked for me, didn't it?

Actually, it didn't. Despite my academic successes, school didn't work for me in ways that truly mattered. The truth is that school, as it's currently structured, doesn't work for *anyone*. And that is true of us, as teachers, as well. So did I lose in learning to conform to the structures of school? To answer that question, I will need to go back in time, to the 1970s.

My Story

I started school as a daughter of immigrant parents who spoke primarily Mandarin Chinese with a smattering of English at home. Still, I had little self consciousness about my English when I attended kindergarten in a working-class suburb of Seattle. As far as I know, this school did not have segregated classrooms for bilingual students. (We were called bilingual back then and later English as a Second Language [ESL] and then English Language

Learner [ELL] and now Multilingual Learner [MLL]). I remember the first two years of school as a vague blur of jump rope at recess, art projects with colorful construction paper, and trading snacks with friends at lunch. In other words—a positive experience.

Then, in second grade, my family moved to a mostly white suburb. By that time, I had enough fluency in English to be placed in a Gen Ed class as I was at my former school, but I was one of the few Asian American students in my Gen Ed class in this new school. Most Asian American children, who looked like me and spoke like me, were segregated into a bilingual program.

To give some context, this was the late seventies and early eighties—a time when many immigrants were from Asian countries of Cambodia, Vietnam, and Korea. This was also a time that the nationalist and racist narrative of "Yellow Peril" was widely perpetuated in the US. I cannot begin to describe the damage of this othering narrative on Asian American children, and the educational segregation of many of us into bilingual classrooms only substantiated this narrative of Asian Americans as foreign, different, and other.

The Asian students in the segregated bilingual program had different lunch and recess periods, except for one recess period where they were "allowed" the same recess as the Gen Ed students. As a Gen Ed student, I dreaded all the other recesses and looked forward to this one inclusive recess as the highlight of my entire day. This was the recess where I wasn't one of the only Asian American students and where I would have some protection from being bullied. It was the one recess where white children were less likely to surround me and tell me to "go back to China." At the time, I didn't understand why they laughed when I replied, "I'm half America! Half China!"

It was only later that I realized those white children were laughing at my English. My Asian friends in bilingual classes were harassed even more severely. We all got the message loud and clear—for Asians, inclusion and belonging was something to be earned. Speak out, speak imperfectly, speak at all—and we will be separated and marked as different. We had to be model students to have a chance of belonging. This is the lesson we learned from the system that separated and marked us.

Most of us learned that lesson well, but I had one friend who resisted. Sara, a bright and energetic girl with a friendly smile, was an immigrant from Cambodia who was placed in a segregated bilingual program. One day, during PE class, my friends and I were being mocked with racial slurs as usual. And as usual, our PE teacher ignored the bullying. I'm not sure what made that day different, but Sara couldn't take it anymore. She began to swear at the top of her lungs at the racist bullies. The rest of us stared at her with our mouths hanging open in shock and delight. For one glorious moment, someone was standing up to injustice and standing up for *all of us*. A thrill ran up my spine... but it didn't last long.

The PE teacher who had ignored the racism we had endured all year was suddenly charging over to us. I'll never forget what he yelled at Sara. "I'm tired of you kids thinking you can get away with stuff just because you're foreigners! You're going to pay the consequences this time!"

The thrill I felt at Sara's boldness quickly dissolved into cold horror. But even then, I recognized the sheer inequity at play here. What about the white kids who bullied us? They had been getting away with racial slurs with no punishment. But, of course, Sara wasn't white. She was hauled off to the principal's office and suspended—just for speaking up against injustice and racism.

Later, Sara ended up transferring to another school, and I lost touch with her. Sometime during high school, I caught wind of a rumor that Sara had dropped out of high school. I was shocked and sad to hear this news about my bright, fierce friend. At the time, I did not think to connect the racism she experienced or the failures of the educational system to this heartbreaking outcome, but now I cannot help but see it. Until our schools address systemic racism, they will continue to fail students.

As a result of these experiences, I learned to be afraid of not speaking perfect English—and not just because of the bullies. I was afraid that if I did not speak perfect English, I too would be confined to those bilingual classrooms with the students who looked like me and spoke English like me—to be marked as even more different when to be different was dangerous. I began to speak as little as possible, petrified that a teacher would call on me or that I would be required to work with a group of my peers. When I was called on, made to read out loud, or required to interact with peers—I sometimes couldn't actually speak. My throat would seize up, my face would flame up, and my whole body would break out in sweat.

I began to see my English as a broken, inadequate thing that kept me from being human in the eyes of my teachers and classmates. This fear lasted all throughout my school years. My teachers all had the same question: Why don't you ever participate in class? I did not know the answer then. I thought that I was naturally timid and socially inept. I thought the failure was all mine. Now I know that it was not my fault. It was the fault of educational policy.

My "failure" at school began to manifest in other ways. I never actively resisted classwork, but at the end of the day, I'd put my homework in my backpack, sneak it home, and stuff it behind my bedroom dresser. I'd show my parents my empty backpack, claim that I didn't have any homework, and proceed to read a book or play outside.

Many years later, when I was in high school, my mother discovered this pile of homework behind my bedroom dresser, by this time, a stack of yellowing paper that reached almost the top of the dresser. "What *is* all this?" she exclaimed, not even noticing the blank worksheets and unfinished addition problems as she tossed them into the recycling bin.

Of course, my habit of hiding my homework caught up with me much earlier than that. At every parent–teacher conference, my teachers always said I was perfectly behaved (except for a lack of participation) and definitely capable of doing my schoolwork—I just didn't do it. My parents and teachers tried bribery and threats, but no extrinsic reward or punishment motivated me to do my schoolwork. I wasn't *trying* to disappoint them. In fact, I wanted more than anything to wake up one morning with the secret sauce to being a good student.

Everyone believed that a good student was somewhere in me, buried by laziness or stubbornness and just waiting to come out. I was as clueless as everyone else as to why I couldn't force myself to sit down and write sentences about Jane and her dog Spot on neatly lined paper or copy down vocabulary lists. Yet I had no problem reading book after book for hours on end or filling up spiral-bound notebooks with stories about enchantresses and warrior girls. I began to wonder if there was something wrong with me. What other reason could there be for my failure to participate or succeed as a student?

Here is what I know now.

Nothing was wrong with me. I wasn't lazy or stubborn. I wasn't a bad student. I simply learned in a way that my classrooms were not designed to accommodate. And my English was never broken. Neither was the English of my Asian friends segregated into bilingual classrooms. *We* were not broken. *We* did not need to be fixed. It was an unjust educational system that was and still is broken and that must be fixed.

What I needed then, and what students need now, is an educational structure that teaches us that there are many different forms of English and English speakers, different learners, and diverse identities—all valued and included.

If our schools are to be equitable rather than unjust, then we need a system based on strengths rather than deficits. For example, take my earlier example of America/American and China/Chinese: "I'm half America! Half China!" In Mandarin, the noun form and adjective form for these words are the same. There is no difference in language between the noun for country and the adjective of belonging to that country. The "mistake" that I was teased for came from my *understanding* of language—not my ignorance of language.

I am reminded here of April Baker-Bell's work in her book *Linguistic Justice: Black Language, Literacy, Identity, and Pedagogy*. Her fieldwork with Black students revealed that the students she interacted with had internalized the belief that Black English was inferior to White Mainstream English (WME). However, Baker-Bell used an "Antiracist Language Pedagogy" (63) to "challenge, interrogate, unlearn, and work toward dismantling Anti-Black Linguistic Racism" (64). To do so, she explicitly uses the term WME rather than "standard" or "correct" English. She also presented the history of resistance to anti-Blackness in the construction of Black English and discussed the complex linguistic rules of Black English as a legitimate language, framing her students' knowledge of Black English as a strength, not a deficit. This critical examination disrupted students' negative feelings about Black English and empowered students to see their languaging as an important part of their racial identity.

That's what I needed at the time—to disrupt my negative feelings about myself and see my languaging as an important part of my racial identity. Now, I can see the empowerment in languaging and identity. For example, the Mandarin word for Chinese Muslim is just one word and one character: Hui. This understanding of language allows me to understand the intersectionality of my identity as a seamless whole rather than as two separate identities of "Chinese" and "Muslim." However, WME does not allow me to express my intersectional identities as one interwoven identity.

In regard to the playground bullying, it was not my *own* limits but rather racism and the limits of WME that caused those kids to make fun of me. I understood the racism, but I did not understand the empowerment in language and identity. Instead, I internalized the shame of my "mistake" about "China" and "America" for years because my education was deficit-based rather than anti-oppressive.

Now, many years later, little has changed. Educational structures still seek to fix what is *not* broken in students rather than fixing the broken structures that persist in segregating students and further entrenching them in inequity.

To be clear, when I criticize segregated MLL or special education classrooms based on a deficit model, I do *not* mean dual language immersion or ethnic studies programs that celebrate students' languages and cultures as strengths. Such programs are a necessary part of structural equity and should not be confused with segregated programs that seek to "fix" students. Strength-based ethnic studies programs actually do invaluable work in countering dominant messages and nurturing students' heritage and cultural identity. In fact, as a Chinese American student, I found that one of the hidden costs of school was the loss of my familial language. To this day, I regret that. I wish my education had valued all aspects of my culture and identities.

When I talk to students now, I hear that same desire in students to have all facets of learning, culture, and identity recognized and affirmed. I believe that is what students need today—a multiple, flexible, equitable, and humanizing framework that honors many ways of learning and *being*.

At the time, I didn't know that was the framework I needed. I believed that the only way to be successful at school was to conform to a flawed system. And that's just what I did. At some point around fifth or sixth grade, school started to become interesting to me, and not coincidentally, I began to do my work and conform to the expectations of school. By the time I reached high school, I was turning in my homework on time, taking honors and Advanced Placement (AP) classes, and earning straight A's. I continued to speak little in class, but it was not considered atypical for an Asian girl to be quiet and studious. Once I started to excel academically, my teachers' concerns melted away. The fact that school continued to be a site of casual racism or that I didn't truly feel a sense of belonging was seldom taken into consideration as a measure of my success.

I had learned to conform, and for me, that meant fully assimilating into a predominantly white high school. It did not matter that I stopped speaking my familial language. It did not matter that I lost myself in painful shyness and self-doubt. The machine of traditional education had succeeded in shaping me into a uniform mold, and as a result, the little girl who so gleefully and willfully colored outside the lines was all but gone.

What I needed was an Anti-Oppressive UD framework to free me from the machine that creates conformity and shame so I could find that joy and freedom in learning again.

Merging the Frameworks for Anti-Oppressive Universal Design

Both anti-oppressive education and UDL are powerful tools for educational equity on their own, but together they can create a transformational framework for equity and for freedom. This process of merging the frameworks is a natural and intuitive one since there is already some overlap in the principles of UDL and anti-oppressive education. Both frameworks are based on equity—anti-oppressive education focuses on the necessity of dismantling inequitable structural barriers, while UDL emphasizes the importance of classroom design for equitable access.

Both frameworks are also based in multiplicity—UDL is grounded in the principles of multiple means for learning, while anti-oppressive education affirms and sustains the multiplicity and intersectionality of cultures, identities, experiences, and representation. By putting these two frameworks together, we are able to create more expansive and layered principles of equity and multiplicity.

Combining these frameworks also allows us to bring in the principle of flexible design from UDL as well as the principle of humanizing pedagogy from anti-oppressive education. We need both the humanizing power of anti-oppressive theories and the concrete emphasis on flexible design in a new Anti-Oppressive UD framework.

This new Anti-Oppressive UD framework provides teachers and students with a practical blueprint for building education under the principles of *multiplicity, flexible design, equity*, and *humanizing pedagogy*. So, let's get started on merging the frameworks of UDL and anti-oppressive education to build the *foundation, principles*, and *purpose* of a new Anti-Oppressive UD framework!

To use a geeky reference, I visualize the merging of the UDL and anti-oppressive education frameworks being like the process that Tony Stark (AKA Iron Man) uses. Those of you who are Marvel Cinematic Universe (MCU) fans will know what I mean. In a typical invention scene, Tony Stark will work with virtual schematics, pulling multiple charts and graphics literally out of thin air. At some point in the process, he'll strip down a framework into its basics, pull out the core components, overlay it over some other framework, spin it around a few times—and ta-da! He's suddenly invented a quantum time machine.

We might not get a quantum time machine (actually, we definitely won't), but we will get an Anti-Oppressive UD framework that can be transformative for our teaching, our students, and ourselves. In other words, it's time to channel our inner superhero inventor and merge our UDL and anti-oppressive education frameworks.

Let's start with our UDL framework.

There's a lot of important concepts in the UDL framework, but we don't need all of them for our Anti-Oppressive UD framework. The foundation of the UDL framework is learning sciences and UD. As discussed, we won't be using learning sciences, but we can extrapolate the principle of *multiplicity* from the more specific UDL principles of multiple means of learning.

We also need the foundational piece of UD. The foundation of UD guides us in the *flexible design* of *equitable* curriculum, practices, policies, assignments, and assessments that have practical and concrete application for teachers. Now, we have the principles of multiplicity, equity, and flexible design.

Here's where we get to be superhero inventors. Imagine taking out the foundational piece of UD and the principles of *multiplicity, equity,* and *flexible design* from a hologram of the UDL framework and setting these aside for later. It's now time to swipe away the schematics of the UDL framework. UDL is a fantastic framework, and it has given us an important model of how to merge UD with another framework (learning sciences), but we are ready to do our own merging of frameworks now.

For the next framework, we're going to use anti-oppressive theories, so let's pull up a virtual schematic of this anti-oppressive framework. The anti-oppressive framework is the one that we'll be using as the base for our new merged framework, so we'll be leaving most of it in place and adding crucial pieces from UDL in order to create the Anti-Oppressive UD framework.

The Foundation, Principles, and Purpose of Anti-Oppressive UD

We'll start with the foundation of *anti-oppressive* theories such as antiracism, anticolonialism, disabilities justice, and intersectionality. Now, we're going to do our first merge! Remember that foundational piece of *UD* that we took from the UDL framework and set aside? Let's slot it into the anti-oppressive foundation, right next to our anti-oppressive theories. Great! Our foundation is now an Anti-Oppressive *UD* foundation.

Next, we're going to merge principles. In our anti-oppressive framework, we have the principles of *multiplicity, equity,* and *humanizing pedagogy*. We're going to take the principles of *multiplicity* and *equity* from the UDL framework and lay them over those same principles of multiplicity and equity in the anti-oppressive education framework—this merge allows us to deepen and enrich those principles of multiplicity and equity.

Then we're going to grab the principle of *flexible design* that we took from the UDL framework and slot it next to the other principles of multiplicity, equity and humanizing pedagogy. Now, we have a nicely robust set of four principles: *multiplicity, flexible design, equity,* and *humanizing pedagogy*.

Now that we have our merged *foundation* of anti-oppressive theories and UD as well as our four merged *principles*, we can create a new *purpose* for the Anti-Oppressive UD framework. The purpose of our Anti-Oppressive UD framework needs to be grounded in anti-oppressive theories, so let's start by looking at the overall purpose of anti-oppressive education: to dismantle systems of racism, colonialism, anti-Muslim hate, antisemitism, economic injustice, ableism, sexism, heterosexism, and transphobia in education. This emphasis on dismantling the oppressive structural barriers that keep us from our full humanity is important—and it is just as important to creatively and intentionally *design* and build new educational structures that are *multiple, flexible, equitable,* and *humanizing* so that we can all be free.

Putting this all together, here is the purpose for the Anti-Oppressive UD framework: To dismantle educational oppression and to design curriculum, practices, policies, assignments, and assessments for freedom.

Without further ado (and please visualize this brightly lit up and spinning in midair for maximum dramatic effect), here is our Anti-Oppressive UD Framework! Please refer to Figure 1.1 for a graphic of this framework.

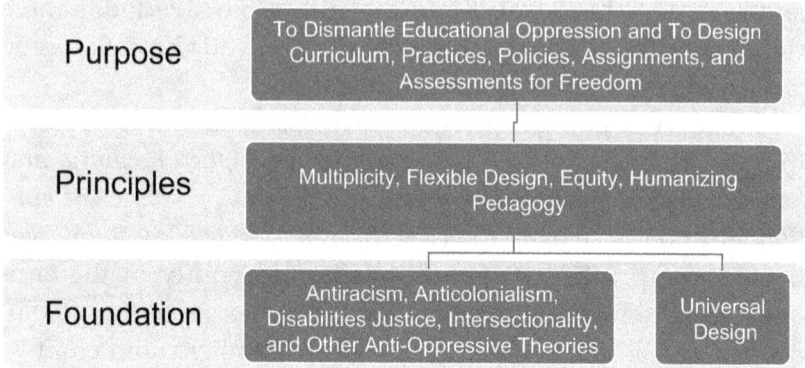

FIGURE 1.1 Anti-Oppressive Universal Design Framework.

The Anti-Oppressive UD framework is exciting to me because it provides teachers with a blueprint to design equitable education that students need to find joy and creativity in learning and to be free to be their full authentic selves.

The following chapters will go into more depth about designing with the principles of multiplicity, flexible design, equity, and humanizing pedagogy as well as the specifics of using the Anti-Oppressive UD framework to design equitable classroom curriculum, practices, policies, assignments, and assessments. Before we end this chapter, however, I want to talk about the need for new tools in building Anti-Oppressive UD.

The Need for New Tools

> The master's tools will never dismantle the master's house.
> –Audre Lorde

I hope it is clear by now that the traditional school structure is not working—and that it needs to be dismantled. However, as Audre Lorde, Black feminist scholar and poet, says, we cannot use the tools of an oppressive system to change that oppressive system. That means we cannot use the same hierarchical, punitive, deficit-based, conformity-focused tools to achieve educational equity.

The tools we use to dismantle inequitable barriers and to design intentionally equitable education must come from our Anti-Oppressive UD principles. In other words, they must be

- Multiple
- Flexible
- Equitable
- Humanizing

An Anti-Oppressive UD Teacher Toolkit

I'm providing a teacher toolkit *example* and an *exercise* at the end of each chapter. The examples and exercises can serve as tools meant to dismantle educational inequity and build new frameworks for equity. When you reach the end of the book, you will have a set of new tools you can use to design sustainable teaching that is multiple, flexible, equitable, and humanizing. My hope is that you will create a toolkit of new Anti-Oppressive UD tools based on the concepts in this book.

Chapter 1 Teaching Toolkit Example

I find it helpful to provide students opportunities to share about themselves in a student survey. These surveys are not only an information-gathering tool but a way for teachers to understand our students and show them that we are interested in who they are. In other words, student surveys can provide a humanizing connection.

My own previous student surveys, however, were focused on collecting information about skills, experience, and needs. For example, I would ask questions about what writing classes students had taken and what writing skills they wanted to improve upon in my class. There is nothing wrong with those types of questions, but when I thought about the purpose of my survey, I realized that I wanted it to do more than just collect information. I wanted it to be a tool to help me design equitable education under the principles of multiplicity, flexible design, equity, and humanizing pedagogy.

That new purpose meant I had to redesign my student survey as a way to understand how I could break down inequitable barriers through multiplicity and flexible design, how I could empower students in their own learning, and how I could build humanizing relationships with my students. That's why I redesigned my survey to focus on students' own goals for their learning and to understand who they are as learners *and* as humans.

As with all my teaching toolkit examples, please take this as an example and not a template! Feel free to modify or use it in any way that is helpful. This example is a student survey for an English class.

EXAMPLE OF A STUDENT SURVEY

1. What name would you prefer to use in this class?
2. What are your pronouns? (For example: she/her, he/him, they/them)
3. What do you want out of this class?
4. What are your interests or hobbies?
5. What kind of books do you like to read and/or shows or movies do you like to watch?
6. What kind of writing do you like to do best? (For example: journaling, fiction, poetry, creative writing, emails/texts with friends, opinion writing, argument essays, research papers, humorous writing)
7. If you could make any creative work you wanted, what would it be? (For example: novel, picture book, painting, choreographed dance, movie, comic book, song, sculpture)
8. Is there anything in the design of class policies, curriculum, practices, assignments, or assessments that might be a barrier for you?
9. What do you need to have a positive experience in this class?
10. Is there anything else you'd like me to know?

My colleague Cathryn Cabral does a beautiful job of humanizing her student surveys by including a series of thoughtful questions that ask students to share about their educational experiences. Her questions don't mention oppression specifically. Instead, she asks students if they've always felt heard and understood in their education, and the responses she gets are moving and illuminating. Here are a few of the questions Cathryn asks, included here with her permission.

> **CATHRYN CABRAL'S SURVEY QUESTIONS**
>
> 1. Share a brief paragraph (3–5 sentences) about your prior educational experiences by addressing some of the following questions:
>   - Have you always enjoyed school? Have you been successful in school? What have you loved about school?
>   - Have you felt seen and understood by your teachers?
>   - Have you been bored in / by school? Has school just been one of those things you had to do? What have you hated about school?
>   - What do you wish school had been for you? What was missing from school for you?
>   - How have your prior experiences in school impacted your thoughts / feelings about being here in this class?
> 2. What do you wish teachers knew about you as a person and / or as a student? (3–5 sentences)

 ## Teacher Toolkit Exercise: Examining Our Own Educational Experiences

In this chapter, I shared my own story, and it has been extremely useful to examine my own educational experience and how school hasn't worked for me. In fact, this reflection has helped me understand how I had become conditioned to accept inequitable educational practices. So, to begin this examination, I'm going to ask you the same question I asked my students and that I answered myself.

- ♦ **Prompt**: How did classroom **structure, policy**, teaching **practice, curriculum, assignments**, or **assessments** create a barrier in your learning or access to education in your K-12 experience?
- ♦ **Directions**: Take some time to either list those experiences or free-write on your experiences. Once you finish, your teacher toolkit will contain an examination of the ways school hasn't worked for you in your educational journey.

What This Tool Is for: You can use this tool to recognize the harm of inequitable educational practices and to consciously undo these practices.

Works Cited

Anyon, Jean. "Social Class and the Hidden Curriculum of Work." *Journal of Education*, vol. 162, no. 1, Jan. 1980, pp. 67–92.

Baker-Bell, April. *Linguistic Justice: Black Language, Literacy, Identity, and Pedagogy*. Routledge, 2020.

Berne, Patty. "Disability Justice - a working draft by Patty Berne." *Sins Invalid: An Unashamed Claim to Beauty in the Face of Invisibility*, Sins Invalid, 10 June 2015, www.sinsinvalid.org/blog/disability-justice-a-working-draft-by-patty-berne. Accessed 19 Oct. 2024.

CAST. "About Universal Design for Learning." *CAST*, Cast, Inc., 2023a, www.cast.org/impact/universal-design-for-learning-udl. Accessed 8 May 2023.

CAST. "A Timeline of Innovation." *CAST*, Cast, Inc., 2023b, https://www.cast.org/impact/timeline-innovation. Accessed 8 May 2023.

CAST. "Universal Design for Learning Guidelines version 2.2." *CAST*, Cast, Inc., 2023c, https://udlguidelines.cast.org/. Accessed 8 May 2023.

CEUD. "About Universal Design." *Centre for Excellence in Universal Design*, CEUD, 2024a, universaldesign.ie/about-universal-design. Accessed 19 Oct. 2024.

CEUD. "History of Universal Design." *Centre for Excellence in Universal Design*, CEUD, 2024b, https://universaldesign.ie/about-universal-design/history-of-universal-design. Accessed 19 Oct. 2024.

Crenshaw, Kimberlé. "The Urgency of Intersectionality." *YouTube*, uploaded by TED Talk, 7 Dec, 2016. www.youtube.com/watch?v=akOe5-UsQ2o. Accessed 7 June 2023.

Freire, Paulo. *Pedagogy of the Oppressed*, 30th Anniversary Edition. Continuum International, 2003.

Gunn Allen, Paula, editor. "Introduction." *Spider Woman's Granddaughters: Traditional Tales and Contemporary Writings by Native American Women*. Ballantine Books, 1990.

hooks, bell. *Teaching to Transgress: Education as the Practice of Freedom*. Routledge, 1994.

"In the White Man's Image." Directed by Christine Lesiak. American Experience, PBS, 2007.

Lorde, Audre. "The Master's Tools Will Never Dismantle the Master's House." *Sister Outsider*. Crossing Press, 2007.

Ma, Diana. "What Is Anti-Oppressive UDL?" Dianamaauthor.com, 11 Nov. 2022, https://dianamaauthor.com/what-is-equitable-udl/. Accessed 18 Nov. 2024.

2

Designing Classrooms for Freedom

Before I read bell hooks' *Teaching to Transgress: Education as the Practice of Freedom*, I was sure that I would never be a teacher. Both my parents were teachers, and I saw the soul-crushing way that the American education system had treated them. They settled for teaching because of the stability it offered, but they lacked passion for their not-quite-chosen profession. After seeing my parents' experience, I vowed that I would never follow in their footsteps. The last thing I wanted to be was a joyless teacher churning out endless worksheets and scantrons.

But the incomparable hooks, Black feminist author, scholar, activist, and teacher, opened up a completely different way to be a teacher. In her book, hooks lays out the ways in which the traditional educational systems uphold white supremacy—the same white supremacy that had shaped my parents' experience and mine in damaging ways. She argues that our teaching practices need to transgress supremacist norms embedded in our educational systems in order to set both teachers and students free from systemic injustice and experience the classroom as a site of excitement and pleasure.

Now, *that* was the kind of teacher I wanted to be.

I loved hooks' ideas of "engaged pedagogy" to make the classroom into a site of excitement and "pleasure" and her argument that such liberatory education requires "a full recognition of the fact that there could never be an absolute set agenda governing teaching practices. Agendas had to be flexible, had to allow for spontaneous shifts in direction" (7). In other words, no teaching to restrictive templates. These were exciting ideas, but I wasn't ready yet to become a teacher.

I did not know how to bring hooks' ideas to life. How can teachers use intentional design to create structures that would allow for the freedom and pleasure that hooks describes in her book? This chapter, in many ways, is a response to that question, but back then, I didn't have an answer.

Instead, I entered a graduate writing program, but I was silenced and marginalized in those writing workshops where participants and even faculty suggested that I make my main characters white for "more universal appeal." That experience convinced me that there was no room for stories like mine—stories about Chinese American protagonists.

Fortunately, I received a teaching assistantship, which not only paid for my tuition but also introduced me to the profession I fell in love with. While I came to dread my writing workshops, I found myself looking forward to the time I got to spend with my students in the classroom. It was no wonder then that I decided to use my tuition waiver to start taking classes at my college's teacher certification program.

One of the first classes I took was an instructional design course. From the first day, it was clear that my professor was an old-school "by the book" kind of teacher. He believed in teaching to a template and required us to follow the directions of each paper *exactly*. There was no room here for flexibility or creativity.

The students who did no more and no less than the objective summaries and observations the assignment called for got fairly good grades. The students who demonstrated original analysis, focusing on the overall course objectives rather than the rigid assignment requirements, got lower grades for not following directions.

I got my second-ever B on a writing assignment in this class, and other students, whom I knew to be accomplished writers and thoughtful, engaged students, did even worse. Most of them dropped out, but I decided to stick it out because I needed this class for my teacher certification. I adopted the strategy of writing my papers in the middle of the night when I was bleary-eyed and too exhausted to have any original ideas, and when one accidentally slipped out, I mercilessly deleted it. My strategy worked, and I got A's on the rest of the assignments.

But then came the last assignment. For this one, my professor told us that we wouldn't be required to follow his restrictive templates. Instead, we were going to design our ideal classroom, and the only requirement was that our design had to be based on a solid educational theoretical framework.

I immediately perked up, and a feeling I had yet to experience in this classroom jolted through me. *Excitement.* Of course, my professor provided a list of suggested texts, all fairly traditional and conservative, but he did say that we could use a text not on his list as long as he approved it.

You can probably guess which text I wanted to use.

I raised my hand and asked if I could use bell hooks' *Teaching to Transgress: Education as the Practice of Freedom* for my paper.

"Never heard of it," he replied, "but I'll take a look and evaluate it."

The next day, I brought my beloved copy of the book to class. I was afraid my professor wouldn't be able to get beyond the title, or bell hooks' name in all lowercase, or the back matter that describes the book as "full of passion and politics" and explicitly names "racism and sexism in the classroom" as obstacles to learning.

Instead, he gave it a cursory glance, flipped it over to the back cover, and, ignoring everything else, placed a finger on the Routledge logo and said, "It's published by an academic press. Okay, you can use it."

I was glad that I could use hooks' book, but I was still worried. After all, my professor hadn't looked at anything beyond the publisher, so he actually had no idea what kind of book he had approved. Nonetheless, if I was being asked to design my ideal classroom, hooks was the only educational theorist that I could imagine using for this essay.

For this assignment, I didn't write the paper in the middle of the night right before it was due. Unlike the other assignments, this one had my full investment, and I spent a lot of time and energy designing an ideal classroom that reflected the values I was passionate about. I wrote about engagement, collaboration, the need for a diverse curriculum, de-centering teacher authority, and, of course, education as resistance to racism and sexism.

By the time I submitted my paper, I felt good about what I had written, but I was less optimistic about the grade I would be getting. Did I make the right decision?

I could have churned out another paper that would have gotten me an easy A, but it wasn't the grade that mattered. It was the opportunity to actually learn something meaningful and express myself authentically that was important. Still, it bothered me to know that all my hard work could result in a poor grade, just because my deeply held beliefs ran counter to my professor's own deeply held beliefs.

About a week later, the professor started class by saying he would be handing back the graded papers at the end of class. He then launched into a lecture that pretty much countered every single one of the values I wrote about in my paper. It felt as if he was delivering his lecture to me personally. I didn't think I was imagining this, because he often paused to stare at me as he emphasized particular points.

My stomach dropped. This did not bode well for my grade.

My professor finished his lecture right before class ended and started handing back papers. I sat in my seat, my whole body clammy with nerves as the other students got their papers back. As usual, there were a lot of mutters and groans.

Finally, my professor reached the end of his stack, and the other students started filing out... but I still hadn't gotten my paper back yet.

What was going on? Gathering my courage, I approached my professor. I took a deep breath and said, "Excuse me, but I didn't get my paper."

He peered at me. "That's because I left your paper in my office. I had it out so I could use it for my lecture today."

Great. I knew I hadn't been imagining it. His lecture *was* meant to argue against the points I had made in my paper.

My anxiety ballooned as I followed my professor back to his office to retrieve my assignment. What grade was he going to give me? Many of my graduate school friends had gotten C's and worse from this professor's class. It wasn't inconceivable that he would fail my paper.

When we finally reached my professor's office, he plucked my paper from his desk but held onto it instead of giving it to me right away. I couldn't see the grade, but I could see the margins filled with red ink and half of my sentences underlined. It looked less like feedback and more like notes. He hadn't been kidding when he said he was using my paper to prepare for his lecture.

Looking me right in the eye, he asked, "You know that we fundamentally disagree on everything, don't you?"

I mentally kissed my chances of passing this class goodbye. With an effort, I kept my voice steady. "Yes. I know."

He handed me my paper. "But it's well written, so I had no choice but to give you an A."

Weak with relief, I took the paper. I had escaped relatively unscathed with a story to tell that would underscore my points about the flaws of conservative traditional education.

Or so I thought.

Designing My Ideal Classroom

At some point, I told my friend and colleague this story and wrapped up by saying, "And when I looked over the paper, every page was marked up with a ton of questions and counter arguments!"

I was expecting my friend to be appalled, but instead she said, "It sounds like your professor took your ideas seriously by entering into inquiry with you."

"Huh." I regarded her in surprise. "I never thought of it that way before." But the more I considered her response, the more I realized that my friend (as she usually is) was right.

I sat there, pondering this new insight. It dawned on me that not only was it rare for a professor to engage in such deep inquiry with a student, but the actual *assignment* was, in and of itself, unusual.

In fact, I couldn't remember any other time I had been asked to design my ideal classroom based on theoretical frameworks that spoke to my own values.

Wait a minute. Was it possible that this assignment nearly thirty years ago from a conservative professor was the only time I was asked to design my ideal classroom using frameworks that mattered to me?

Yes. It was.

Teachers are often asked to come up with assignments and assessments to fit preset standards, but we are seldom asked to consider anything but district or state outcomes in designing our classes. Sometimes, we design our classroom policies too, but again, those policies are seldom based on our own values or teaching philosophies and more often on set school or district policies. Most likely, there are already boilerplate policies from everything from tardiness to academic dishonesty that we are encouraged to use for our own classes.

I no longer have my old paper to refer to, but I have a hunch that most of the policies, assignments, and assessments I created over the years bore little resemblance to the ones I designed for my ideal classroom. As teachers, many of us learn quickly that our own ideologies or individual strengths matter less than how well we uphold outcomes and standards.

This is particularly pertinent to me as a BIPOC (Black, Indigenous, and People of Color) woman. I understand that I am valued because I'm a box my school can tick off on their diversity checklist, but not necessarily valued for my actual cultural identity or the lived experience I bring to the classroom. I know that my "diversity" is valued only as long as I continue to conform to the norms and expectations of my school, and I am not alone in this.

I have heard many stories from other BIPOC teachers who are hired for the diversity they bring to the school but discouraged from bringing our whole authentic selves into our teaching. Schools should encourage BIPOC teachers to bring all of our multiplicity into the classroom even if (or maybe even *especially* if) this necessitates a change in system values. Instead, however, evaluations and improvement plans are often used to shape our teaching into the mold of what the institution already values—education based on white, patriarchal, cisgender, heteronormative ideals.

This, unfortunately, is true for most of us as teachers. What matters is not our uniqueness but our ability to conform. In this way, we are mired in the same oppressive system as our students. But what if it could be different? What if, instead of teaching to conform and to reinforce conformity, we teach to dismantle injustice and empower our students?

That is exactly what we can do by using Anti-Oppressive Universal Design (UD) in our classes. I've had years of designing to adhere to larger state and district standards, but I am now coming back to where I started—designing a classroom for pleasure and freedom.

It occurs to me that there is yet another takeaway from my story. Although teachers come from all different places on the political spectrum (as my professor and I did), classroom *design* offers us a starting point for conversation. This is useful to consider since teachers do not work independently. We are part of departments and schools made up of other educators who might even "fundamentally disagree" with our ideas about education. However, what we *do* have in common is the desire to design classrooms that nurture our students' learning. Sometimes, finding that point of connection is as simple as asking other teachers what they do to design classrooms that nurture students' learning… and also what keeps them from that goal.

Standards and the Design Process

I often talk to committed and impassioned teachers who are frustrated by the restrictions of standardized curriculum and prescriptive practices. They want to meet their students' specific needs, goals, and interests, but instead, they are hampered by a district-mandated curriculum that asks them to cover the topics deemed important by the school district rather than what is important to their students.

It's true that teachers cannot ignore the reality of standards. In fact, many states have adopted Common Core State Standards (CCSS) that set student outcomes for each grade. Fortunately, while the widely used CCSS does emphasize benchmarks for student learning, it also de-emphasizes the means to reach those benchmarks—leaving flexibility for teachers to develop a curriculum that is multiple, equitable, and humanizing.

In fact, in the introduction of a document on the Washington State English Language Arts (ELA) Learning Standards (which are aligned with CCSS), one of the headers is actually labeled "A focus on results rather than means" ("CCSS in ELA" 4). The ELA Standards document continues by stating, "By emphasizing required achievements, the Standards leave room for teachers, curriculum developers, and states to determine how those goals should be reached and what additional topics should be addressed" ("CCSS in ELA" 4). This means that the standards do not control the *ways* we teach, so we can design flexible means for our students to meet those standards.

Yet state learning standards are sometimes cited as the reason teachers must adhere to district-mandated curriculums. This is an unfortunate way that learning standards have been implemented. Sadly, I have talked to some teachers who left the profession because they felt like they had been reduced to machines churning out instruction based on a set curriculum with no room to center student engagement and empower students to make their own choices about their education.

But wouldn't it be wonderful if we were free to design a classroom that is responsive to our students' needs and interests and sustains their diverse identities and cultures? The good news is that we can use the Anti-Oppressive UD principles of multiplicity, flexible design, equity, and humanizing pedagogy to free our students and ourselves from set curriculums and prescriptive practices; we can design a classroom that not only supports our students in meeting learning standards but empowers students to express their creativity and their full authentic selves.

Since learning standards actually *do* allow for flexibility in how teachers design their classrooms, there is no real justification to force teachers into a "one size fits all" pathway towards the standard. District constraints are a very real concern for teachers, but the problem lies with rigid district-mandated curriculum rather than a standards-based curriculum. The truth is that we *can* design a classroom that supports students in meeting learning standards and loosen the mandates that restrict our teaching and our students' learning—by using Anti-Oppressive UD principles of multiplicity, flexible design, equity, and humanizing pedagogy.

In fact, the main problem with a standards-based curriculum has less to do with the standards themselves and more to do with the belief that students with marginalized identities, like BIPOC, lower-income, and disabled students, *cannot* meet the standards. This is a limiting belief—it limits students from learning and coming into their full selves, and it limits what we can do as teachers.

Unfortunately, the harm of these limiting beliefs on students is devastating. As one student explained in response to a survey on structural barriers:

> Being the only black student has its struggles, and I felt singled out and felt I was responsible for carrying the knowledge of my race. When I wasn't able to understand concepts (as we mainly taught ourselves), I was put into a box of being incapable since my race was 'lazy.'

However, if we believe that all students *can* meet the standards as long as we design our curriculum with multiplicity, flexible design, equity, and humanizing pedagogy, then we can empower students to be successful in their learning and to be free to develop authentic expression, creativity, and ways of being. That is a wonderfully hopeful and creative place to start.

So, let us begin the work of designing our classrooms as places of equitable and joyous learning in collaboration with our students. This chapter will discuss how students can be free to learn and grow into their full selves in a classroom designed with

- ♦ Multiplicity of means of teaching, student choices, and diverse representation
- ♦ Flexible and intentional design of classroom structures to support student freedom and learning

- Equity-minded design of classroom structure
- Humanizing pedagogy in the design of the classroom structure

This chapter will go into more depth about the four Anti-Oppressive UD principles I introduced in Chapter 1, so I want to provide a fuller explanation of these principles here, defined with more context and a more comprehensive purpose. These four principles will be the cornerstones for this chapter and all the chapters that follow.

Principles of Anti-Oppressive UD

1. **Multiplicity**: Multiplicity of options in policies, curriculum, practices, assignments, and assessments to acknowledge and dismantle expectations of conformity based on racist, ableist, colonialist, classist, sexist, heteronormative, and other oppressive norms. Multiplicity of diverse and intersectional representation to affirm and sustain students' cultures and identities.
2. **Flexible Design**: Flexible design in curriculum, practices, policies, assignments, and assessments to free students and teachers from the rigidity and punitive nature of oppressive educational structures and to create structures of support rather than confinement.
3. **Equity**: Equity-minded design of curriculum, practices, policies, assignments, and assessments to break down inequitable structural barriers that students of color, disabled, lower-income, trans, and other marginalized students face and to create full access for all students.
4. **Humanizing pedagogy**: Teaching and learning to affirm students' and teachers' full humanity in resistance to the dehumanization of educational oppression. Relational, community-centered, collaborative, and responsive structures and practices meant to sustain cultures, identities, and authentic expression of self.

These are the actual principles I wish I had been able to articulate in that long-ago "Designing an Ideal Classroom" paper. I no longer remember what I wrote for that assignment, but most likely, that essay was full of grand ideals (Not that there's anything wrong with ideals!) and light on concrete design structures and implementation. However, I know that, as a novice teacher, I often had a tough time translating my educational ideals into the classroom. That is why the design part of Anti-Oppressive UD is so important. Intentional design allows us to create solid support structures for our students to learn in multiple and flexible ways.

This chapter is focused on design because there might be the assumption that a classroom based on the principles of multiplicity, flexible design, equity, and humanizing pedagogy is a bit of a free-for-all and loosey-goosey at best—and out-of-control and chaotic at worst. In fact, I think my professor may have written something to that effect in the margins of my essay.

I certainly have gotten some dubious reactions when I say that I want to design my classroom for freedom. But here's the thing about intentionally designed classrooms—they have structure. The point of a classroom designed for freedom is not to get rid of all structure—the point is to intentionally design structures that scaffold our students' learning and support their freedom to be their full authentic selves.

That means these structures cannot be designed to be rigid. I want to stress that structure is *not* synonymous with rigidity. Anti-Oppressive UD is a framework to design classroom structures that support students, to guide and scaffold learning, and to provide multiple and flexible ways they can demonstrate learning standards. So, with that in mind, I would like a redo on my "Designing an Ideal Classroom" assignment!

Designing My Ideal Classroom with Anti-Oppressive UD

Imagine a classroom where students walk into class knowing they are free to be themselves and that I, as their teacher, recognize their humanity. In this classroom, the student knows they can tell me that they are having a rough day and don't feel like engaging or that they are having a wonderful day because their team won a soccer championship. Either way, they know that I will be responsive.

For the student having a rough time, I would empathize with the student and reassure them that the class activities are flexibly designed, pointing out options already built into the class structure for accessing that day's materials (to be discussed in Chapter 4 "Building Equitable Classroom Policies with Anti-Oppressive UD"). For the student who won the soccer tournament, I would celebrate their win and perhaps recommend a soccer-themed book or story they might enjoy as an option for an upcoming assignment where students can choose their own text to read.

In fact, it is important to me to affirm the multiplicity of student identities. In middle and high school, students are figuring out who they are, and I want my classroom to support them in those journeys and in those identities. That is why I structure my class to center the multiplicity of diverse representation so that the texts and stories students read are by BIPOC, LGBTQ+, disabled, Muslim, and Jewish authors and that there is a multiplicity of stories that include ones of joy and resistance. (I'll talk more about this in Chapter 3, 'Building Equitable Curriculum and Practices with Anti-Oppressive Universal Design'.)

In my ideal classroom, students are not all required to do the same thing because multiple options are deliberately built into the classroom structure. For example, in an English class, students might have the following options:

1. In a group of 3–4 people, discuss the author's main argument and supporting evidence in this article.
2. Working independently, write a reflection on the author's main argument and supporting evidence in this article.

It is important to note that although these practices are multiple and flexible, they are also practices *intentionally designed* into the class structure to support student choice and freedom. A classroom designed for freedom is not unstructured or chaotic.

A classroom designed for freedom is built with intentional and transparent scaffolding in place.

Here's one example of a Universal Design element I put into my classroom. Many years ago, I took a class on supporting MLL (Multiple Language Learners) students and learned that it was a helpful practice to put the day's schedule on the board because some MLL students can understand more in writing than they can through listening.

I thought this was a great idea and started doing this for all my classes, and I soon discovered that putting the daily schedule on the board was useful scaffolding for pretty much *all* students, not just MLL students. Some neurodivergent students told me the daily schedule helped them focus if they knew what to expect. Many students told me that they liked to be able to know what they would be doing every day. The schedule actually ended up being useful scaffolding for *me* as well in terms helping me keep my lesson on track.

These are just a few examples of supportive and responsive classroom structures deliberately designed with Anti-Oppressive UD, and I will dive into these in more detail in the upcoming chapters. For now, I will give just one more example of an intentionally designed support structure.

For this chapter on design, I wanted to write a teaching philosophy based on what I would say to my students if I had to explain the beliefs that motivate my classroom design.

In the Teacher Toolkit at the end of the chapter, I will provide an exercise for you to write your own statement of teaching beliefs and hopes to guide your classroom design. In the meantime, here is my statement about how my beliefs and hopes guide my classroom design.

My Teaching Beliefs and Hopes

I believe that every student is capable of learning, and I am committed to supporting each student in their individual journey to be successful in meeting the learning outcomes of this class. I recognize that there is no one way to meet the learning outcomes of the class, so I have designed the class so that the ways to meet those standards are multiple, flexible, and responsive to student interests, needs, and different ways of learning.

I also believe in designing student-centered curriculum and practices. The class is designed to be supportive and flexible, so if anything in the design or structure of the class isn't working for you, then please let me know so we can collaborate to make it accessible. I believe in designing the class in collaboration with students to create an equitable classroom that recognizes and accommodates individual student needs. I also believe in working together to build a classroom where both learning and teaching are sustainable. I believe in the importance of diverse representations and that all students, particularly those with underrepresented identities, should see themselves reflected in a multiplicity of stories.

It is my hope that, throughout this class, you will grow together into a community of learners who support each other. I also hope that this class will be a place for you to express yourself fully, feel affirmed in your cultures and identities, freely explore new ideas, joyously develop your creativity, and have fun!

My statement of "Teaching Beliefs and Hopes" is what guides me in my designing class to be multiple, flexible, equitable, and humanizing. I find that being open about these ideals with my students encourages them to share their own beliefs and hopes about their education.

The Power of Student Stories

In designing for freedom, it is important not only that we share our own teaching beliefs and hopes but that we are responsive to what students say about their own learning. To show the importance of responsive teaching as well as the Anti-Oppressive UD principles in practice, I'd like to share a student story. Student stories have not only shaped my own classroom design practices, but have encouraged me to keep revising my classroom design to be flexible and responsive to shifting student needs.

Over the years, I've heard many heartbreaking stories about the educational injustice students have experienced, so it is important for me to include student stories in this book. To tell these stories, I will be using the method of composite character counterstorytelling to represent multiple students. The purpose for composite character counterstorytelling is to use multiple voices to counter dominant narratives about marginalized students.

I first learned about composite character counterstorytelling from April Baker-Bell's excellent book *Linguistic Justice: Black Language, Literacy, Identity, and Pedagogy*. Baker-Bell uses composite characters "to counter majoritarian myths and narratives that get perpetuated about linguistically and racially diverse groups in education" (44). In other words, her decision is based on a resistance to essentializing her students' experience and instead creating a fuller representation of the educational injustice Black students encounter. It is important to note that Baker-Bell emphasizes that her composite characters are *not* fictional in that the students she describes do actually exist and the experiences she narrates really did happen (44). She describes her methodology of creating composite characters through "interview transcripts, field notes, research memos, artifacts, and other research data" (44).

My students and my methodologies, of course, differ from those of Baker-Bell. My composite student character counterstories come from my conversations with students, personal narrative essays, and student surveys. The teachers in these student composite character counterstories are also composites based on my own teaching experience, interviews with K-12 teachers, and teachers whom students have described as helpful or unhelpful.

Like Baker-Bell's characters, my student composite characters are not fictional. My composite characters are based on real students and their real experiences with real teachers.

Kyle's Story

Kyle is a disabled student who was placed into a self-contained special education classroom from the moment he started school. His school decided that he was incapable of reading or writing, so they didn't even try to teach him. None of Kyle's teachers attempted to design the curriculum so that he could meet the standards and learn how to read and write. Instead, Kyle spent his days bored out of his mind—either coloring or cutting paper or simply staring at the wall, waiting for the day to end. There were only a handful of tasks he was deemed capable of, and none of them engaged or challenged him. As he put it, he had been "thrown away and left to rot."

Kyle was desperate to be taught something... anything, but every year, his hopes dwindled. By the time he reached high school, he was severely depressed. He had become resigned to the fact that school would never be a place of learning for him.

The problem, of course, was inequitable educational structures and design. Kyle's school had a policy of putting all the significantly disabled students into a segregated special education classroom that was not designed for learning. There's a lot wrong with this approach, starting with the obvious (to me anyway) fact that segregation, by its very nature, is inequitable. Also, self-contained special education simply does not work. Kyle spent most of school consigned to boredom and nonexistent expectations in a segregated classroom, which was the worst possible way for him (and *any* student) to learn.

Again, the problem was *not* an internal deficit. The problem was the education system that sees disabled students and students with marginalized identities as having deficits that can only be "fixed" with inequitable status quo solutions like educational segregation. Kyle's school saw his inability to conform to their model as a deficit in him rather than the model itself. It didn't seem to matter that the model didn't work and was based on racist and ableist segregationist ideology and historical oppression.

Unfortunately, Kyle's story is not unique. Disabled students are often segregated into special education classrooms or pulled out of class for special support/social-emotional skills/study skills sessions to help develop whatever it is that they "lack." Again, schools need a shift in thinking about how they think of marginalized identities. Disabilities have nothing to do with what a student can or cannot do. It is about students like Kyle being disabled by systems of oppression that try to change them and do not allow them to be their full authentic selves. Sadly, it is this deficit-model thinking that is baked into the foundation of educational design.

Happy for Now

Fortunately, Kyle's story did not end there.

Kyle refused to accept his school's assessment of his limitations. If his school refused to believe him capable of anything but coloring and cutting paper, then he would teach himself. More than anything, he wanted to learn how to read and write. He loved the stories he saw on TV and in movies and dreamed of writing his own stories someday. Kyle knew he had to learn how to read and write first, but how was he to do that? He had no access to curriculum or anyone willing to teach him. All he had was his incredible will and ingenuity.

Determined to learn what his school kept telling him that he couldn't, Kyle got transcripts of the shows he loved. Then he started matching up the words on the transcript to what he was seeing and hearing.

Incredibly, that is how he taught himself how to read and write.

This led to Kyle finally being placed in a Gen Ed creative writing class his senior year with Ms. Lee, a teacher who understood how to design multiple, flexible, equitable, and humanizing curriculum and practices to reach every student.

Kyle was delighted to be in a Gen Ed high school class and even happier that it was creative writing. He loved the storytelling in the shows and movies he watched and was interested in telling his own stories. However, he became increasingly agitated as Ms. Lee referenced story after story as an example of the kind of writing they would be doing in class. Kyle had never heard of any of these stories or books and had no idea what Ms. Lee was talking about when she explained scene building. Since many students, like Kyle, needed visuals to follow the lesson, Ms. Lee was using a slideshow presentation with graphics as she verbally explained the story concepts. Usually, these kinds of visuals helped Kyle understand the lesson, but they weren't helping him this time.

Finally, Kyle interrupted Ms. Lee and blurted out that he had never actually read a story or a book since he had taught himself how to read and write through TV shows and movies. In the brief pause before Ms. Lee responded, Kyle's mind began to race. What if she reprimanded him for interrupting her lesson? That was how his teachers usually responded to his questions when he forgot to raise his hand and simply said what was on his mind. Then Kyle remembered that Ms. Lee was different. She had responded to his interruptions before by briefly validating his thoughts or questions and asking him to wait until she was done because she didn't want to forget her own train of thought. Ms. Lee made it clear that she was asking him to wait because of her own needs and not because she was judging him for interrupting her.

This time, however, Ms. Lee *did* pause her lesson to respond in the moment. "That's amazing that you taught yourself to read, Kyle." She regarded him thoughtfully, and Kyle's heart began to sink, not because his teacher seemed upset, but because of what he suspected would come next. In the past year, Kyle had been assigned many short and basic readings below his grade level to make up for what he "lacked." In fact, he had learned more about penguin habitats from these readings than he ever cared to know. Teachers often gave him repetitive and boring tasks with the well-intentioned purpose of helping him learn, but these tasks never engaged him. He simply couldn't learn from such mundane rote work.

However, to Kyle's astonishment, Ms. Lee simply said, "Actually, that makes total sense. I can see that you have a unique cinematic writing style. Tell me about the movies and shows that you're interested in." She listened closely as Kyle described the fantasy and science fiction shows he watched, and she affirmed that this was a great way to learn character development and scene-building. Then she went on to teach the lesson with examples from TV shows and movies in addition to stories and books.

Kyle began to relax. Finally, he was not only interested in the topic matter but also understood the lesson Ms. Lee was teaching.

Then the worry crept back in. Ms. Lee might be willing to engage him and adapt her lessons, but what would happen when it came time to also write? He knew that he didn't have the best grasp on punctuation or other rules of grammar, and he still wasn't sure he could write a short story or even wanted to. No one else in the class seemed to have a problem with the short story form they were being taught, so he was hesitant to bring up how difficult he was finding the assignment to write a short story.

Fortunately, Kyle felt comfortable enough with Ms. Lee to talk to her about his concerns, and Ms. Lee thanked him for communicating with her. Then she suggested that he write a screenplay instead of a short story since a screenplay would meet the assignment's storytelling objectives as well as a short story would. Kyle was happy with this option and eagerly set out to write a screenplay for a fantasy short film.

Kyle was able to breathe another sigh of relief when his first assignment was graded. In Ms. Lee's assessment of his work, she gave feedback on where his cinematic style worked and how he could bring those descriptions and scene-building to other parts of his screenplay—leaning into his strengths instead of calling out his deficits. In fact, as Kyle read this feedback, what he was feeling wasn't just relief… it was actual excitement about his writing.

Multiple Means of UDL

This story shows us the importance of multiplicity, flexibility, and student-centered design. That framework not only gave Ms. Lee structure for designing her classroom with multiple means but also allowed for the flexibility to respond to Kyle's needs with multiple means.

Kyle's story demonstrates just how concrete and useful the *multiple means* from the UDL framework are in creating equitable access for students, and we can see the three principles of multiple means at work in his story. Under the first principle of *multiple means of engagement*, Ms. Lee took the time to listen to Kyle and engage him in the lesson by asking about his interest in movies and TV shows. She also used the second principle of *multiple means of representation* by using both a slideshow presentation and verbal explanation in her lesson on point of view and scene-building. Finally, Ms. Lee used the third principle of *multiple means of action & expression* by giving Kyle the option of a different assignment to write a screenplay instead of a short story so he could demonstrate his strengths while still meeting the objectives of the assignment.

Kyle was able to learn effectively, fully meet the standards of the class, and gain confidence in his writing because his curriculum was being designed and delivered through the multiple means of UDL, which is based on learning sciences. However, a framework built on a foundation of learning sciences does not directly address the harm of ableism that years of segregated special education had inflicted on Kyle. UDL provides equitable access in an educational system built upon ableism, racism, colonialism, economic injustice, and sexism, but it does not directly address the root causes of those inequities. A truly powerful and transformative educational framework needs to be built on a foundation of anti-oppression to break down an oppressive system and empower students and teachers.

In other words, we need an Anti-Oppressive UD framework. It was actually Ms. Lee's understanding of ableism and disabilities justice that allowed her to use the principles of UDL in an anti-oppressive way and to merge the principles of multiplicity and flexibility with the principles of equity and humanizing pedagogy. When Ms. Lee used *multiple means* of *engagement, representation*, and *action & expression*, she did so with the understanding that the barriers Kyle was experiencing were not the result of what he could or could not do but to the ways that the educational system disabled him.

Therefore, she knew she had to change the design of her teaching practices, assignments, and assessment rather than try to "fix" Kyle. That's why she focused on fixing the educational design of her teaching and her class. Importantly, Ms. Lee's teaching was not based on her assumptions of what Kyle could or could not do because of his disability. Whenever something wasn't working, Ms. Lee assumed that the problem was with the educational design—and not with the student.

Again, Ms. Lee built her teaching upon a foundation that recognizes educational oppression and the harm it has done in order to use the principles of multiplicity, flexible design, equity, and humanizing pedagogy to dismantle inequitable barriers. She knew that Kyle could not gain access to equitable education unless his teachers explicitly resisted the oppression that had prevented him from accessing his education.

Ms. Lee was aware that, until his senior year, Kyle had been denied access to Gen Ed because his school had decided that his "deficits" made him unteachable. There was little she could do about problems with the larger school structure, but there was still much she *could* do in the classroom. That was why she rejected the conformity and deficit thinking of traditional education and instead taught with the Anti-Oppressive UD principles of multiplicity, flexible design, equity, and humanizing pedagogy.

It was not just multiple means but the more comprehensive Anti-Oppressive principle of *multiplicity* that was evident in Ms. Lee's teaching when she affirmed Kyle's multiplicity of storytelling instead of holding his storytelling to the standards of a single, restrictive structure. She was also teaching with the principle of *flexible design* when she redesigned her lesson to incorporate examples from movies and television, which benefited not only Kyle but other students as well.

Ms. Lee was also aware of the inequity of holding students to white-centric norms of language as well as Kyle's inequitable educational experience, so she was grading with the principle of *equity* when she graded on Kyle's strengths in writing rather than marking him or her other students down for their writing mechanics. Finally, Ms. Lee was teaching with the principle of *humanizing pedagogy* when she recognized Kyle's interruptions as part of his neurodivergence and interacted with him in a responsive way. Instead of dehumanizing him by exerting her authority and punishing him for interrupting her lesson, Ms. Lee simply acknowledged him and asked him to wait if it was not a convenient moment to address his question or comment, recognizing his humanity and needs. In this, she was also considering her own humanity and needs as a teacher as well as the needs of the rest of the class.

Kyle's story shows that it was not any internal "deficit" that kept him from learning but rather the inflexible and inequitable *design* of his education that restricted his learning. Anti-Oppressive UD design is not set in stone. In this framework, design is iterative and responsive—developed in relationships with students and changing with student needs.

Once Kyle was in a classroom intentionally designed with Anti-Oppressive UD principles, the educational structures that once contained him were rebuilt into structures that scaffolded his learning so that he was able to express his whole authentic self *and* fully meet the class standards. In other words, Kyle was able to learn in a classroom designed for freedom. Kyle's story is just one example of how all students can succeed under the Anti-Oppressive UD principles of multiplicity, flexible design, equity, and humanizing pedagogy—not only in their learning but in becoming more fully themselves.

Anti-Oppressive UD to Dismantle Conformity and Deficit-Thinking

During a conversation with a student in my creative writing class, I was reminded of why Anti-Oppressive UD is so necessary. Cora was an Indigenous and dyslexic student, and I had asked to meet with her because it was clear that some of the assignments were not working for her. I'd had Cora in a class before, and I knew she was meticulous in reading everything I assigned, including the optional readings. She also made sure to ask me questions about anything she didn't quite grasp until she had a firm understanding of the concepts. Cora's writing was gorgeously lyrical and achingly powerful, and she almost always wrote more than was required in her assignments. At the time, she was working on an absolutely beautiful piece of writing about language, Indigenous culture, and loss under colonialism.

However, when it came to the writing prompts from the craft book we were using, it was obvious that Cora was stuck. Even though these responses to the craft book prompts were not evaluated and students had the option to ignore the prompt, her responses were punctuated with concerns about whether she was doing it "right." When we met, Cora told me that she just didn't understand the different points of view described in the craft book or why adjectives were to be used sparingly or what adjectives even were.

"Why don't we go about this in a different way?" I replied. "You are an amazing writer, and it's clear that these assignments have become a barrier to your writing. The prompts in the craft book are meant to help you write, but you don't need that. In fact, these prompts are blocking you. The best thing for you to do is to ignore them."

Cora stared at me. "But don't I need to learn this stuff? I think I'm missing some of the basics, and that's why I'm struggling." She had been failed by the education system and had to teach herself to read as an adult. "I can try harder to figure it out. Maybe I can read some more supplemental materials." She seemed despondent at the thought.

"The problem isn't you," I replied. "The problem is that the craft book isn't working for you, and you certainly don't need to put more effort into it! This book might have some useful explanations and tips, but as we discussed, these concepts are based on Western narratives and ideas of craft. You are drawing from Indigenous narrative and craft traditions for your writing, which is wonderful. I love your writing, and I would hate for you to change your incredible and necessary writing into something that you're told it's supposed to be."

Cora nodded. "I think I understand what you're saying."

"Good," I said. "Then let's focus on what you need to develop your writing. Instead of following the craft book prompt, continue working on your piece. Take whatever is useful from the readings and lessons and ignore the rest. Remember, the guiding question shouldn't be—what do you need to learn to make your writing fit a certain structure? It should be—what will help you realize your own vision for your writing?"

Cora took a deep breath. "Okay. I can do that. Thank you. I always think I'm doing something wrong and beat myself up when I just can't get it."

It broke my heart that she thought she or her writing was "wrong" in any way. I knew that Cora was aware of the way ableism and colonization had profoundly damaged her educational experience. Yet she was still susceptible to the harmful messages of deficit and conformity.

"Can you do something for me?" I asked. "If you get frustrated with a reading or assignment in the future, will you come and talk to me about it? You can assume that the problem isn't you… because it's not. Instead, assume the problem is with the assignment or whatever isn't working for you because we can fix *that*."

"Yes. I'll try." Cora gave me a tremulous smile and put her hands to her heart. "I know there's this script inside me that tells me I am broken and need to be fixed. I need to unlearn that script."

I felt a ping of recognition at her words. I knew that script too, and although few students verbalize it as clearly as Cora, I knew that many of my students had that internal script as well.

In thinking over that conversation with Cora, I wondered how different it might have been if something in her educational experience (or mine, for that matter) had disrupted the harmful messages of the conformity and deficit models. Maybe then we wouldn't default to thinking that our struggles in school were the result of a lack of effort or grit. Wouldn't it be great if we understood our challenges to be the result of unjust educational systems? But instead, we are taught to focus on fixing our own deficits.

I was reminded of the shame I felt in using the language of "Half China, Half America" and how April Baker-Bell used "critical consciousness-raising" (63) to disrupt her students' shame in their language and identity to empower them.

I realized that we need a critical consciousness-raising tool to "unlearn that script," as Cora put it. So, I developed a tool to do just that in the form of a lesson plan and will share it with you in the toolkit below.

Chapter 2 Teaching Toolkit Example

This is an example of a lesson that you might use to help students understand what educational barriers are. Often, schools implement interventions like productive persistence, growth mindset, social emotional learning, and improving study skills to encourage students to adapt to the structures of school. *This lesson, however, is not meant to help students adapt to school.* In fact, it is the antithesis of those types of traditional education interventions. This lesson is meant to help students recognize the structural barriers of school and to counter the narratives of conformity and deficits. In fact, you might think of this lesson as an Anti-Oppressive UD intervention!

Anti-Oppressive UD Intervention

Objectives

- Students will understand the concept of structural barriers.
- Students will identify the structural barriers to their own education.
- Students will recognize the challenges they face in their own education to be a result of structural barriers rather than individual deficits.

Learning Activities

Part 1: Reaching Educational Goals

1. **Pre-writing Reflection**: Ask students to write for 5 minutes on the following prompt: *What do you want from school? What can you do to reach those educational goals?*
2. **Sharing Out**: Ask students to raise their hands if they wrote about how working on their behaviors would help them reach their educational goals. (Give examples of what you mean by "working on their behaviors," like

being on time, turning in work, paying attention in class, making more of an effort, improving organization, and gaining study skills). Put the tally on the board and say you'll come back to this.
3. **Discussion**: Ask students: *What were some challenges you had in working on those behaviors?* Most likely, students will talk about how difficult it is to make behavioral changes. Then ask: *Did anyone write about advocating for the class structure to change instead of changing yourself to help you reach your educational goals?* Most likely, few, if any, did. Make the transition to talking about structural barriers.

Part 2: Understanding Structural Barriers

1. **Defining Structural Barriers**: Define structural barriers. Here is the definition I give: *Structural barriers are design elements built into institutions (like school, legal system, and healthcare) that limit people's access.*
2. **Defining Privilege in the context of Structural Barriers**: Here is a definition I give of privilege. *Privilege (like white privilege, male privilege, or class privilege) is an unearned advantage that can help get you past those structural barriers. Think of it as an automatic door opening for you.* Here, I might give an example of a student being able to afford a test prep class for the SATs because of class privilege. I would also point out that college admission tests are a structural barrier that isn't good for *anyone* even if its effects are sometimes eased by privilege.
3. **Defining Oppression in the context of Structural Barriers**: Here is a definition I give of oppression. *Oppression (like racism, sexism, or economic injustice) is an unearned disadvantage that makes those structural barriers even worse. Think of it as an extra security gate slamming down over the locked entrances.* Here, I might give the statistic that Black students are suspended three times as much as white students because of structural racism (ACLU, "School-to-Prison Pipeline [Infographic]"). I would also make it clear that school suspension isn't good for *anyone* but that its effects are often made worse by oppression.

4. **Why This Matters**: Explain that we might not be able to do anything about larger structural barriers like college admission tests and school suspension, but we can do something about the structural barriers that exist in the classroom. Make clear that a structural barrier has nothing to do with individual characteristics or skills. If a cement wall exists where a door should be, then no amount of grit or effort is going to get you past that wall. A structural barrier is a limitation built into the design of the classroom policies, curriculum, practices, assignments, and assessments. In other words, a cement wall.

Part 3: Empowering Students

1. **Putting It Together**: Tell students that you are coming back to the topic of changing behaviors to reach educational goals. Summarize the previous discussion of how changing behaviors will not remove a structural barrier. Emphasize that the only way to remove a structural barrier is to change classroom design, *not* individual student behaviors.
2. **Post-writing Reflection**: Ask students to think about the previous discussion about structural barriers. Give examples of classroom policies, curriculum, practices, assignments, and assessments. Ask students to write for 5 minutes on the following prompt: *What classroom policies, curriculum, practices, assignments, and assessments (not your own individual behaviors or characteristics) have created structural barriers that keep you from reaching your educational goals?*
3. **Sharing Out**: Ask students to share the policies, curriculum, practices, assignments, and assessments that have barriers in them. List the responses on the board/slide.
4. **Defining the Principles of Anti-Oppressive UD**: Define the principles of multiplicity, flexible design, equity, and humanizing pedagogy. Here are brief definitions of each that you can use. These are based on the principles I shared

earlier but worded in a slightly different way to focus on the structural barriers part of the lesson.
- ♦ **Multiplicity**: Multiple options in policies, curriculum, practices, assignments, and assessments to break down the limitations of conformity and standardization.
- ♦ **Flexible Design**: Flexible alternatives in policies, curriculum, practices, assignments, and assessments to break down the rigidity of educational structures.
- ♦ **Equity**: Differentiated policies, curriculum, practices, assignments, and assessments to break down the inequitable structural barriers explained by the automatic door and security gate metaphor. Again, this is a metaphor for an unjust system because those with privileged identities get the automatic door, and those with oppressed identities get the security gate. Equity counters the equality mindset of treating everyone the same regardless of the automatic door and security gate system. Equity recognizes the injustice of the automatic door and security gate system.
- ♦ **Humanizing pedagogy**: Teaching and learning to affirm everyone's full humanity in resistance to the dehumanization of oppressive structural barriers.

5. **Discussion**: Ask students: *How can we create multiplicity, flexibility, equity, and humanization in these policies, curriculum, practices, assignments, and assessments to remove structural barriers?*

Teacher Toolkit Exercise: Designing Teaching Beliefs and Hopes

This is an exercise to support you in writing your own "Teaching Beliefs and Hopes" statement! I provided an example of my own statement in this chapter, but yours, of course, will be different because it will be based on your *own* beliefs about and hopes for your teaching.

Note that this is probably not the place to discuss your belief in the importance of the Oxford comma or the belief that the quadratic formula should be memorized. Instead, this is an opportunity to intentionally design a statement to express what you find meaningful about teaching and to be supportive of your students.

- **Prompt**: What are your beliefs for and hopes about your teaching?
- **Directions**: Take some time to either list your beliefs and hopes or write about your beliefs and hopes in paragraph form. If you are feeling stuck in getting started, you might want to begin a sentence with "I believe" or "I hope".

What This Tool Is for: You can include your "Teaching Beliefs and Hopes" statement in your syllabus to provide a supportive foundation for the classroom and to provide a humanizing lens to who you are as a teacher with your unique beliefs about your teaching and hopes for the classroom and for your students. This statement can also serve as a touchstone for designing curriculum and practices.

Works Cited

ACLU. "School-to-Prison Pipeline [Infographic]." *ACLU Multimedia*, ACLU, 2024, www.aclu.org/issues/juvenile-justice/school-prison-pipeline/school-prison-pipeline-infographic. Accessed 19 Oct. 2024.

Baker-Bell, April. *Linguistic Justice: Black Language, Literacy, Identity, and Pedagogy*. Routledge, 2020.

"Common Core State Standards for English Language Arts and Literacy in History/Social Studies, Science, and Technical Studies." PDF. *Washington Office of Superintendent of Public Instruction*, 2011, ospi.k12.wa.us/student-success/resources-subject-area/english-language-arts/english-language-arts-learning-standards. Accessed 22 Oct. 2024.

hooks, bell. *Teaching to Transgress: Education as the Practice of Freedom*. Routledge, 1994.

3

Building Equitable Curriculum and Practices with Anti-Oppressive Universal Design

When I first outlined this book, I thought of curriculum and practice as two separate chapters. This had much to do with how curriculum is often framed—as an immutable structure that teachers labor under. Curriculum, in this traditional education model, is unaffected by individual teacher practices, but this rigid structure is exactly what we are trying to free ourselves and our students from—and we can do that through multiple, flexible, equitable, and humanizing curriculum design and teaching practices.

In other words, teaching practices designed to be responsive to and sustaining of students' cultures, identities, needs, and interests shapes and are shaped by flexible and equitable curriculum design. This chapter will discuss how curriculum and practices that are designed for freedom:

- ♦ Center the multiplicity of diverse representation
- ♦ Create multiplicity through flexible curricular design

♦ Create student-centered and humanizing practices that are *responsive* to and *sustain* students' cultures and identities, interests, and needs

To provide some framing for this chapter, I'd like to share a student's perspective about curriculum and practices. At the end of a class that specifically discussed both the reality of and resistance to oppressive educational structures, I conducted a student survey. The response below is to the following question: "How did classroom *structure*, *policy*, teaching *practices*, *curriculum*, *assignments*, or *assessments* create a barrier in your learning or access to education in your K-12 experience (especially in middle school or high school)?" In my student Nicki's survey response, she wrote the following:

> There was a distinct lack of diversity at my high school that led to several curricular issues. In my US History class, there were no trigger warnings or discussions of offensive language when learning about the history of Black people in America, which led to many students (of all races) becoming triggered and sometimes crying in class or while doing homework. Lack of diversity training also led multiple teachers to committing egregious microaggressions and disregarding feedback from students of color.

Centering the Multiplicity of Diverse Representation

Nicki's response highlights a common and deeply troubling problem in curriculum design. Too often, the experiences of BIPOC (Black, Indigenous, and People of Color) people as well as of other marginalized groups are either *not* represented at all or are underrepresented, misrepresented, or limited to histories and stories of oppression. These lessons are taught almost as an add-on to the curriculum rather than built into the foundation of the curriculum. For example, the history and stories of Black people are often relegated to a unit during Black History Month in February and limited to histories and stories about slavery, segregation, and anti-Black laws and violence.

This is a problem because, as author Chimamanda Adichie explains in her TED Talk "Danger of a Single Story," to tell a "single story" about a marginalized group flattens the multiplicity of people's experiences and reduces the experience of a whole group to a single narrative. In this case, the curriculum of Nicki's US History class perpetuated the single story that Black histories and stories are *only* about oppression and suffering.

Unfortunately, the danger of this single story is not only students "crying in class or while doing homework." The danger also lies in the history class perpetuating the belief that to be Black is *only* about oppression and suffering and therefore a negative thing. Being Black, of course, is not a negative thing or a problem—it is *racism* that is the problem. And it is racism that also reinforces a single story.

I still remember the time in elementary school when another kid, who was white, confronted me in the school cafeteria to ask me, "Do you eat dogs?"

I just stared at her, horrified by the very idea. My whole face flooded with heat as I stammered, "No… but why are you asking?"

Casually, she replied, "Oh because you're Asian."

Her words were like a blow to my chest. She thought I ate dogs because I was Asian—because of who I *was*. Before I could respond, she asked, "You're not Korean, are you?"

I wasn't sure why it mattered, but I felt I had to answer. "No," I said faintly. "I'm Chinese."

"Good," she said with a smile that made me feel sick to my stomach. "It's Koreans who eat dogs. We can still be friends."

I didn't remind her that we weren't actually friends in the first place. In fact, I didn't say anything at all. Even though I knew my Korean friends were no more a danger to this girl's dog than I was, I remained silent. Instead, I sat there in shame about who I was. I was embarrassed to be so other and foreign that this girl really believed it was possible that I would eat her pet. At that moment, I felt that she saw me as less than human and wondered who else at my school saw me that way.

That is the danger of the single story. It reinforces racist and other oppressive ideology and creates internalized shame in BIPOC students and others with marginalized identities—and it is dehumanizing.

Fortunately, we can design a curriculum that resists and counters the inequity and danger of a single story to affirm students in their full humanity. I should clarify here that although I don't want a curriculum that tells a single story of marginalized people as oppression and suffering, I also don't want to ignore racism and other oppression either. To design for equity, we need to first acknowledge inequity.

For example, learning about the different forms of racism, including internalized racism (where I internalized the dominant negative messages about my own race), would have been helpful to me in understanding that the burden of shame should not have been *mine* when the white kid assumed that Asians ate dogs. It would have also been helpful to understand what was happening—that this kid had a single story of Asians that had nothing to do with the multiplicity of who I was and the richness and wholeness of my culture and identities.

I do understand when teachers admit their hesitations about discussing racism, ableism, sexism, and heterosexism in the classroom. They tell me that they don't feel they know enough to teach these issues. Sometimes, teachers also feel that their disciplines of PE, science, or math don't lend themselves to such teaching. Fortunately, recognizing the realities of oppression does not need to be difficult. I would again recommend, as an important starting point, centering the importance of diverse representation. It would not take much to discuss BIPOC, LGBTQ+, women, and disabled scientists and athletes in science and PE classes or to include diverse representation in math story problems, for example.

By designing curriculums that center the multiplicity of diverse representations, we can counter the danger of the single story. The histories and stories of BIPOC, disabled, LGBTQ+ people should not be relegated to a single unit but should be built into the very foundation of the curriculum. Take Nicki's US History class, for instance. That history class did not have to limit the experiences of Black people to slavery and lynching. If the multiplicity of diverse representation were an important undergirding of the curriculum design, then a US History class could cover, for example, the Harlem Renaissance, cross-solidarity workers' movements, the American Indian Movement, and the overall role of BIPOC people in US History.

In fact, the multiplicity of diverse representation in my elementary school classes might have countered that single story of me as a dog-eater. If we had a richness of stories, histories, and experiences of Asians in my classes, that other kid might have seen me as human. As Dr. Rudine Sims Bishop states, children need the opportunity to read books that are windows into other experiences and also read books that are mirrors, reflecting their own experiences. It is harder to dehumanize someone when we are drawn into their stories of riding dragons, navigating sibling rivalry, and figuring out who they are in the world. It is also harder to see yourself as less than human when you see yourself in stories of embarking on spacefaring adventures, falling in love, and fighting dystopian regimes.

In other words, diverse stories humanize us all. Every child should have the experience of being seen and seeing oneself truly—and not as a dehumanizing and flattened caricature or stereotype. In my classes, I use author interviews, articles, blogs, acknowledgements, videos, and talks to show why marginalized authors write the books they do. So often, authors say a variation of the same thing: "I wrote the book I couldn't find when I was a child. I wrote the book I, myself, needed." Many authors who write for children also talk about how they want their young readers to see themselves in stories.

In fact, that is why *I* write Middle Grade and Young Adult books—because I believe in the importance and necessity of diverse stories and believe that every child should see themselves in the stories they read.

> **WHY I HOPE READERS SEE THEMSELVES IN MY CHINESE AMERICAN YA PROTAGONIST**
>
> Republished from the We Need Diverse Books Blog
> Content warning: Mentions of racism, particularly racism against Asian Americans during the COVID-19 pandemic, including descriptions of physical violence and attempted murder
> Diana Ma was a mentee in the 2019 Mentorship Program and had a Young Adult Fiction Mentorship with Swati Avasthi. To learn more about the mentorship program, visit the We Need Diverse Books website at diversebooks.org.
>
> By Diana Ma

Lately, I've been thinking about belonging. What do home and homeland and citizenship mean for me as a second-generation Chinese American? And how did young adult literature shape my sense of belonging in its depiction of Americanness?

These questions came to the forefront as I was writing *Heiress Apparently*, the first book in an epic and romantic series that follows the descendants of the only female regent of China. The *Daughters of the Dynasty* series begins in modern-day Los Angeles and Beijing, and my main character is also a second-generation Chinese American. Gemma is a struggling actress who gets her big break in a movie shot in Beijing. The catch? For some mysterious reason, her parents have forbidden her from ever stepping foot in Beijing. And Gemma soon suspects that they might have good reasons for this rule.

I had different reasons than Gemma, but I also didn't visit China until I was a young adult. And like Gemma, I've felt uneasy all my life about my sense of belonging both in the US *and* in China. The difficulty of straddling different cultures is a common-enough theme in stories about Asian Americans, so it's natural that belonging would be on my mind when writing *Heiress Apparently*.

But I don't think it's that simple.

Asian Americans' right to belong in the United States has always been challenged. Currently, we are in the midst of the COVID-19 pandemic when anti-Asian racism, harassment and violence have been increasing at an alarming rate. In one recent and horrific incident, a customer at a Sam's Club stabbed an Asian American family, including a 6-year-old and a 2-year-old. The man was attempting to kill them because he thought they were Chinese and infecting people with coronavirus. And this is just one example of the ways Asians have been targeted for our perceived otherness. It's no wonder that I am so deeply invested in exploring the theme of belonging.

In Gemma, I wanted a character who would challenge these ideas of otherness. Gemma is a young Chinese American actress fighting against Hollywood Asian stereotypes: the sex-crazed and nerdy foreign exchange student, the sexless and nerdy straight-A student, the karate-chopping villain, the dangerously sexualized Dragon Lady, or the submissive and sexualized courtesan... In other words, Gemma has a tough road!

Gemma's character is inspired by the many Asian and Asian American actors, writers, and directors fighting for fuller and more diverse representations of our cultures. While this is a time of heightened anti-Asian national rhetoric, it is also a time of cultural resistance. BIPOC artists, in every cultural medium, are creating works that challenge narratives of hate. The filmmaker Lulu Wang, the actor John Cho, and the screenwriter Adele Lim make wonderful films, but just as importantly, they are outspoken about the need for Asian representation and resistance against anti-Asian bias. Gemma was born from their work and their strength. My book wouldn't exist without them.

As a reader, I have always looked for belonging in books. When I was a kid, there weren't a lot of Asian American characters in the books I loved—especially in YA romances. But I kept reading and loving those YA romances. I wanted to lose myself in stories, but I was also looking for how to be a teenage girl figuring out the complexities of crushes, friendships, and family. The first part was easy—I had no problem getting lost and forgetting myself in worlds vastly different from my own. The second part was harder. My YA romantic heroines could not provide me with a roadmap of how to be an Asian teenage girl because their stories were not like mine.

Those white heroines never floundered in the face of microaggressions and racial assumptions—so they could not guide me in figuring out the complexities of my own identity. Yes, white girls in YA romances had their own obstacles to "happily ever after." Maybe she was the dorky journalism club president and he was the football captain. Luckily, clever banter and adorable quirks would win the day, and the couple would realize, "Hey, we're more alike than we thought!" Race was almost never an issue. The journalism club and the football world might collide, but no one had a crisis of identity over it. Those white heroines knew who they were. They were not constantly asked "Where are you from?" and expected to give a one-word answer that would quantify their entire being for the benefit of the questioner.

But as much as I envied those girls for their witty comebacks and confident flirtations, I envied them even more for their friendships. The main character of YA romances always seemed to have a circle of friends or, at the very least, a BFF. Her friends knew her intimately, and they had her back. Sure, sometimes there were misunderstandings, but her friends never told her, "I like you because you're not like other Asians." Like it was a *compliment*.

All those books could teach me was how my life measured up against the lives of fictional white girls. They could not give me what I so desperately needed—stories like mine and characters like me.

This is why I stopped reading YA romances. As I became an adult, I read fewer and fewer YA books in general, but I gave up on romance completely. I just couldn't shake the guilt I felt about wanting to be the girls in those stories. Because if

I had wanted to be those girls, then didn't that mean I wanted to be white? Maybe it wasn't that simple, but a complex knot of shame was enough for me to slam the door on the YA romance genre.

So what changed? After all, I've written a YA romance.

My way back to YA isn't that hard to explain. #Ownvoices YA books by BIPOC writers such as Jenny Han, Angie Thomas, Samira Ahmed, and Anna-Marie McLemore (to name just a few) came on the scene. Children's literature has become more diverse in representation (although there's still a long way to go). It has now become possible for my own children to see themselves reflected in the books they read. And it has become possible for me to write the books I once needed so badly.

This is a day I could have never imagined as a Chinese-American teen trying to find myself in books. Today, my own YA romance comes into the world. I hope the readers of Gemma's story find the belonging they're looking for.

Designing a Standards-Based Curriculum to Be Flexible and Equitable

I realize that an equitable and flexible standards-based curriculum sounds like a paradox, but the reality is that many teachers are required to teach to state or district learning standards, so it is helpful to figure out creative ways to develop a standards-based curriculum. As I mentioned in Chapter 2, while the Common Course State Standards (CCSS) do set benchmarks for student learning, they also de-emphasize the means to reach those benchmarks, leaving room for flexibility.

In addition to allowing for flexible design, a standards-based curriculum does not need to restrict the content of the curriculum. In fact, a standards-based curriculum can leave room for a multiplicity of content choices. As the document for Washington State English Language Arts (ELA) Standards explains,

> While the Standards focus on what is most essential, they do not describe all that can or should be taught. A great deal is left to the discretion of teachers and curriculum developers. The aim of the Standards is to articulate the fundamentals, not to set out an exhaustive list or a set of restrictions that limits what can be taught beyond what is specified herein.
>
> ("CCSS in ELA" 6)

I want to be clear that "a great deal left to the discretion of teachers" does not mean complete lack of restrictions. For example, the language of "curriculum developers" can give school districts leeway to mandate set curriculums. However, it is still heartening to know that the aim of the standards is not to impose a "set of restrictions that limits what can be taught beyond what is specified" in the standards.

What that means to me is that we *can* be creative and go beyond the state or district learning standards. For example, Gholdy Muhammad, in her book *Cultivating Genius: An Equity Framework for Historically and Responsive Literacy*, argues for a set of new literacy standards based on culturally responsive teachings. I agree, and I believe we can design new learning goals that go beyond the state and district ones and support students' full humanity, self-expression, and creativity.

Designing New Learning Goals

As teachers, we often have learning goals mandated by the school, district, or state. I want to recognize the requirement to design curriculum around those learning goals, but I *also* want to encourage expanding the scope of those goals in creative ways. We can use the Anti-Oppressive UD principles of multiplicity, flexible design, equity, and humanizing pedagogy to create a curriculum that empowers students to meet new learning goals that are student-centered and humanizing. Here are examples of what those expanded learning goals might look like:

Students will be able to:

- ♦ Understand the multiplicity and importance of diverse, intersectional representation.

- Demonstrate responsiveness to a multiplicity of cultures, identities, and histories.
- Express and sustain the student's own cultures, identities, and interests in ways that are meaningful to the student.

These are learning goals that can be included with the state standard ones to create a humanizing curriculum. However, simply setting new learning goals is not enough for equity. We also need to design our curriculum so that our students can *reach* those goals. Take the first one about diverse representation. Our curriculum will never be equitable or humanizing to BIPOC, LGBTQ+, disabled students if our texts are limited to white, cis-het (cisgender and heterosexual) male, nondisabled authors.

It's true that we might be limited by state standards, but we can still find creative ways to center diverse identities and build a curriculum for freedom. For example, Washington state ELA standards require 11th and 12th graders to learn about Shakespeare, but teachers can use that as an opportunity to center diverse Shakespeare interpretations like James Ijames's play *Fat Ham*, a queer Black retelling of *Hamlet* set in a cookout in the south; Jane Smiley's novel *A Thousand Acres* novel, a feminist environmental justice retelling of *King Lear*; or Chloe Gong's novel *These Violent Delights* novel, a *Romeo and Juliet* retelling set in 1926 Shanghai.

However, when we focus on building diversity into our curriculum, it's also important to design intersectionality into the foundation of the course. In other words, by centering diverse identities, I don't mean that we should organize our curriculum into single-identity units. In my classes, I intentionally design themed units so that diverse representation isn't divided into single-identity units—such as a unit on Black, Indigenous, Asian, Latine, or LGTQ+ identities. Instead, those identities are represented in intersectional ways and built into the foundation of each unit. None of us is just "one thing," and a curriculum that sorts identities into single identities or single stories is not responsive to our students' whole authentic selves.

By creating themed units instead of single-identity units, I can create both openness and support for my students' shifting identities and relationships. For example, the units of an ELA curriculum could be: "Rewriting the Rules," "Rewriting the Bard's Tale," "Poetry for Joy and Resistance," "Alternate Pasts, Possible Futures, and Other Worlds," and "Fairy Tale Retellings."

Our students are just figuring out who they are at this point—their identities and relationships with family and friends are in flux, so we need to build a curriculum that is responsive and open to support the changes in our students' lives. We need to recognize the intersectionality of our students' identities and of representation. For example, if I had a curriculum organized by single identities, then where would I put a book with a bisexual Asian main character or a book that has an important representation that's not reflected by my limited categories—like an autistic Jewish main character? Or what if students want to read a feminist environmental justice retelling of *King Lear* that doesn't fit into one of the neat boxes of my curriculum? There needs to be room for student-centered exploration and all the complexity and richness of intersectionality.

Coming back to Nicki's student survey response, I think that part of what she might have been responding to in the student survey was that "history of Black people in America" was taught as a separate unit as if the experiences of Black people were somehow separate from the history of the United States. Sometimes, it can feel like the representation of BIPOC and other marginalized identities is treated like a houseguest to our curriculum rather than an innate part of it. We might recognize that we need to include this guest, but instead of intentionally redesigning the household in ways that affirms diversity—not as a guest, but as an integral part of the household—we build a hurriedly constructed add-on. That is not an equitable or humanizing design. Instead, we need a new design that is multiple and flexible—and mindfully and intentionally designed to be equitable and humanizing—integrating diverse representation into every part of the curriculum.

In this chapter's "Teaching Tools Example," I'll provide a sample curriculum that centers the multiplicity of diverse, intersectional representation, builds in learning standards, and creates equitable accessible to all students through flexible design. This curriculum is organized into thematic units, and it's important to note that I'm able to include a large range of books in every unit because I don't expect every student to read the same book. With flexible design, I've created units that support student choice to read the book that speaks to them.

I also wanted to have options for students who might struggle with reading long and complicated texts, so I included a shorter and more accessible book in each. For example, I might include an option of reading a short novel in verse (Walter Dean Myers's *Street Love*, a *Romeo and Juliet* retelling set in Harlem) in the "Rewriting the Bard's Tale" unit. In addition, I include an anthology in each unit that features multiple diverse authors like *That Way Madness Lies*, edited by Dahlia Adler for the "Rewriting the Bard's Tale" unit again.

The positive news is that reading these diverse texts can still meet a variety of broad state standards such as this ELA anchor standard for reading: "Read and comprehend complex literary and informational texts independently and proficiently" ("CCSS in ELA" 35). In other words, we *can* build a standards-based curriculum that incorporates state standards—*and* student-centered and humanizing learning goals that enrich the state learning standards.

Equitable and Humanizing Teaching Practices

In her student survey response, Nicki not only describes lack of diversity and curricular issues but also states, "Lack of diversity training also led multiple teachers to committing egregious microaggressions and disregarding feedback from students of color." Unfortunately, Nicki's experience is far from uncommon. I often hear from students that conformity (even if it is conformity to a harmful curriculum) in schools is the overruling expectation of school. It is not surprising then that when students try to push back on educational oppression, they are ignored or labeled as noncompliant—and therefore a problem.

At the same time, as Nicki points out, teachers are not always provided with any diversity training. First of all, I should say that schools absolutely have the responsibility to provide diversity training for their teachers, yet it is important to acknowledge that schools do not always have the funding for that training. However, it does not require diversity training to simply *listen* to our students.

Listening to our students is a necessary part of designing equitable and humanizing teaching practices. Another important part of this design is to build practices with a solid foundation of anti-oppressive theories. The foundation of Anti-Oppressive UD includes two important frameworks that have helped me design my own equitable and humanizing practices: Culturally Responsive Teaching (CRT) and Culturally Sustaining Pedagogy (CSP).

CRT is a pedagogy based on the belief that students of color learn better when teaching practices include students' own cultural references. Geneva Gay defines CRT as "using the cultural characteristics, experiences, and perspectives of ethnically diverse students as conduits for teaching them more effectively" (106). This is an equitable and humanizing framework that is responsive to the learning of students of color and their cultures.

CSP is a framework that builds upon CRT. In addition to centering students and their cultures, CSP resists the cultural erasure and marginalization of students of color by implementing a pedagogy that sustains the cultures of BIPOC students. As Django Paris and H. Samy Alim explain in their book *Culturally Sustaining Pedagogies: Teaching and Learning for Justice in a Changing World*, "CSP seeks to perpetuate and foster—to sustain—linguistic, literate, and cultural pluralism as part of schooling for positive social transformation" (1). This is a framework that consciously builds equitable and humanizing curriculum and practices to resist the destruction of the cultures of students of color and to sustain those cultures. CRT and CSP both counter the deficit model by affirming marginalized students' cultures as strengths rather than deficits.

It is important to acknowledge that I will be discussing CRT and CSP in the context of the intersectional Anti-Oppressive UD framework. That is, I will be talking about how to use CRT and CSP expansively to design teaching practices that dismantle multiple forms of oppression such as racism, ableism, heterosexism, and transphobia. I also want to note that anti-oppressive design is always done through responsive relationships with students.

Often, students can tell us exactly what they need. Nicki is actually quite specific about two things the students in her US History class needed: "trigger warnings and discussions of offensive language." She also states clearly that students of color *did* give feedback in response to the curriculum and the microaggressions they faced… but that it was disregarded.

Sadly, students have told me that when they have tried to give feedback to their teachers about aspects of a curriculum that they find traumatizing, they have gotten responses along the lines of: "Learning requires discomfort" or "Buck up—you can handle it." In other words, these are classic "grit" responses that assume students need more perseverance or other qualities. These responses might come from the messages teachers receive that it is up to us to toughen up our students rather than designing the curriculum to include trigger warnings and discussions of offensive language.

Yet, being responsive to our students is often not hard to do. For example, if my class were reading a book that includes a scene where a character of color is taunted with racial slurs, I would put in the assignment to read the book a content warning that states, "Depictions of racist bullying." I would also provide multiple options for books to read, including stories of joy with protagonists of color. Naturally, I can't anticipate everything that might trigger students, so I ask students to help identify material that might need content warnings. I frame it as building a community of care for each other. This actually led to students posting content warnings about their *own* writing in online peer workshops without any prompting from me. This was a beautiful example of a practice that students created themselves out of care and respect for each other.

Of course, content warnings are just one example of why we need to listen to what students tell us. We need to listen to our students and value their knowledge, cultures, and identities. We also need practices that affirm and sustain those cultures. For example, when I offer multiple options for books to read, I am deliberate in choosing books with diverse representation so that I am sustaining those underrepresented communities. I also make sure to teach about the importance of diverse books to counter the inequities of underrepresentation and to create positive change.

I believe that CRT and CSP teaching practices are important parts of Anti-Oppressive UD because we cannot affirm students' full humanity if we do not respect, care for, and sustain our students' cultural knowledge and histories. Geneva Gay puts it beautifully when she describes CRT as "a moral imperative, a social responsibility, and a pedagogical necessity" (109).

Equitable and humanizing curriculum and teaching practices informed by CRT and CSP were what Nicki needed to be fully seen and heard in her high school classes, and it was certainly what Holly, another student composite character, needed too.

Holly's Story

Holly was an Indigenous student who had always struggled with completing assignments although she did not have an Individualized Education Plan (IEP) or 504 plan. However, she always passed her classes (seldom with higher than a C despite her teachers all insisting she was bright and capable), and she generally got along with her teachers. The exception was an English class in her junior year.

At first, Holly was excited about the class because her teacher had decided to assign a book written by an Indigenous author. Unfortunately, Holly's enthusiasm was short-lived. During the first lesson of this unit, her teacher asked Holly to tell the class what reservations were like.

This made Holly feel uncomfortable, but she didn't quite understand why. After all, she *was* proud of her Indigenous heritage and eager to share her experiences. Putting aside her uneasiness, Holly talked about the positive aspects of the tribal reservation she grew up on, emphasizing the strength of her tribe's community and culture.

Without warning, her teacher interrupted to contradict Holly in front of the other students. Numb with shock, Holly listened as her teacher insisted that reservations were poverty-stricken and plagued with drug and alcohol addiction. Holly could not believe that her own lived experiences were being negated. She was also mortified to be forced into a limiting identity constructed from ignorance and assumptions. When she tried to speak up for herself, however, her teacher shut her down.

This incident ended up creating emotional distress for Holly and made her feel like an outsider at her school. Later, when Holly talked to a couple of her classmates about how she felt about what her teacher said, they told her they "didn't think it was a big deal" or even that the teacher's "intentions were good." This left Holly feeling so isolated and confused that she not only stopped speaking about the experience but stopped speaking in class at all.

This situation also had a negative impact on her grade. To do what the class discussions and assignments required of her, Holly would have had to conform to a damaging ideology that ran counter to how she saw her own Indigenous identity. She certainly did not learn effectively in that English class and actually came close to failing it. She ended up with a D in the class, which was a lower grade than she had ever gotten.

These were heavy consequences for Holly, and they could have easily been prevented. It was the teacher's lack of culturally responsive and sustaining practices that caused Holly to nearly fail. Although Holly clearly had pride in her Indigenous culture, the teacher saw only the deficits of reservations.

Instead of seeing Holly's culture as a deficit, the teacher could have used CSP to affirm the strength of Holly's culture, acknowledging the poverty as a result of racism and settler colonialism. The teacher didn't need a deep understanding of the legacy of colonialism to avoid harming Holly, but she *did* need to use CRT to listen to and understand Holly's perspective with respect and care.

Happy For Now

Fortunately, Holly had a different English teacher the next year. Ms. Young had a reputation for being a teacher committed to social justice, and Holly was optimistic about this class. She was determined to put last year's experience behind her and start fresh.

It was immediately obvious to Holly that Ms. Young's class was different. For one thing, Ms. Young foregrounded the importance of diverse representation in her class. In addition, even though Ms. Young acknowledged that there was a standard curriculum of readings for senior English, she provided multiple options for assignments and stated that she would be flexible in making modifications as long as students met the standards of each unit.

This statement was put to the test as Ms. Young introduced the unit on environmental justice literature. A student raised his hand to say he had already read the assigned novel and asked if he could read a different one that he already had in mind. Ms. Young immediately approved this alternate book. After class, a friend of Holly's stayed to talk to their teacher about the content of the book being triggering for her. Later, the friend told Holly that Ms. Young had offered her another option. Holly was impressed that although their teacher made sure that students were meeting the standards of the unit, she never questioned a student's reasons for wanting an alternate reading.

But it wasn't until Ms. Young showed Chimamanda Adichie's TED talk *Danger of a Single Story* that Holly understood just how different this class would be. In this video, Adichie talks about how limiting representations are socially constructed and, as the title indicates, how dangerous these "single stories" are. It was at that moment that Holly realized her teacher last year had a "single story" of tribal reservations and Indigenous tribes. At last, she had the language to describe why the experience in her previous English class affected her so negatively.

This revelation was making Holly's brain buzz with new ideas, and she desperately wanted to talk about the connections she was making between Adichie's ideas and last year's experience. However, the dismissiveness she had encountered before made her worried about how her classmates would react now. Still, Ms. Young had created such a positive community of respect and caring that Holly decided she would risk speaking up. Before she could second-guess herself, she raised her hand.

When Ms. Young called on her, it all came tumbling out. Holly told the class that she felt shamed and silenced about sharing her pride in her community and a story about reservations that challenged the single story about Native Americans. Holly could tell at once that her teacher and classmates were moved by her story. Holly ended by saying, "What my teacher said about reservations just didn't describe *everything* about reservations. When she said that all reservations were just places of alcoholism and poverty, it made me feel like what I had to say about my actual life didn't matter. Like I was just a stereotype."

"Beautifully stated!" Ms. Young said. "I'm paraphrasing here, but as Adichie says, The problem with stereotypes is that they flatten people's actual experiences. You've just expressed that so movingly and powerfully, Holly."

Holly smiled. It felt good to have her experiences and feelings heard with no one invalidating her story. The discussion continued with other students sharing their own experiences with having a single story told about them. Holly was amazed. She had been feeling so isolated since the incident last year, and now she was finding out that she wasn't alone.

After the discussion, Ms. Young moved on to talk about the essay assignment for this unit, and Holly started to think about asking her teacher to make a modification to the assigned book. Even though she hadn't already read the assigned book, didn't find any of the content to be potentially triggering, and didn't have anything against the assigned book, she really wanted to write an essay about the importance of an Indigenous story in resisting the danger of a single story.

Holly couldn't remember the last time she had been enthusiastic about a school assignment, so she decided she would ask Ms. Young if she could do the essay for this unit on the book by an Indigenous author that she had been assigned last year. Maybe it could be a kind of do-over. Mustering up her courage, she stayed after class to float her proposal to Ms. Young.

When Holly finished, her teacher looked at her thoughtfully and said, "While I absolutely love the idea of writing your essay on resisting the danger of a single story, the issue is that the book you're proposing doesn't quite fit the theme of environmental justice for this unit."

Holly's heart sank. She had completely forgotten about that requirement.

Then Ms. Young said, "I do have a suggestion that could make your idea work. Have you heard of *Solar Storms* by Linda Hogan?"

She shook her head, wondering where her teacher was going with this. "What's that?"

"*Solar Storms* is a beautiful novel about community, healing from trauma, the connection between women, the importance of cultural traditions, and environmental justice. It's written by Linda Hogan, a Chickasaw author."

Holly's mouth dropped open. How had she never heard of this book? Ms. Young continued to give some content warnings and the information that it was a longer book, but Holly wasn't concerned about any of that. "The book sounds perfect! Can I read it for this unit?"

Ms. Young laughed. "Of course. In fact, I can lend you a copy." Her eyes shining, she added, "I can't wait to read your essay. You're doing really important, powerful work here in resisting a single story of Indigenous culture."

Holly smiled. "Thanks. I think this will be fun, actually." She meant it. For the first time in a long time, she was looking forward to an assignment and interacting with her teacher and peers. In fact, Holly was actually excited about learning and school.

The Power of Anti-Oppressive Universal Design

Because of the multiplicity, flexible design, equity, and humanizing pedagogy that went into the design of the curriculum and practices of Ms. Young's class, Holly had a clear sense that diverse stories were important to resist the dangers of a single story. Just as importantly, she had validation that the educational oppression she experienced was real and that her voice and her stories were important. She also felt empowered to make her own choices in creating a curriculum that spoke to her interests and was meaningful in sustaining her cultural identity.

Holly's story not only shows the power of culturally responsive and sustaining practices, which are crucial to the Anti-Oppressive UD principles of equity and humanizing pedagogy, but also demonstrates the principles of multiplicity and flexible design as well. When Ms. Young created multiple options in her assignments and sustained the multiple cultural identities and experiences of her students, including Holly's, she was designing curriculum and practices under the principle of *multiplicity*. Ms. Young's flexible practice of working with Holly to find a book by an Indigenous author to meet the standards of the unit is an example of the principle of *flexible design*. Ms. Young's overall design of the curriculum to foreground the importance of diverse representation and her practice of centering students' freedom to read books that represent their cultural identities shows that Ms. Young is designing the curriculum and practices with the principle of *equity* in mind. Finally, Ms. Young's responsiveness, valuing of Holly's cultural knowledge, and affirmation of Holly and the other students as fully realized, authentic humans rather than as passive receptacles to be filled with knowledge show her designing curriculum and practices under the principle of *humanizing pedagogy*.

I love Holly's story because it demonstrates how a curriculum designed with Anti-Oppressive UD supports students' freedom to learn and be themselves in the classroom. Her story also demonstrates the importance of teachers being responsive to students. As Holly's and Nicki's stories both show, it's important to listen to students. If we are responsive to our students and committed to sustaining their identities, cultures, and knowledge, then we can create equitable curriculums and practices in anti-oppressive collaboration with our students.

Redesigning Inequitable Peer Writing Workshops

In deciding how to approach curriculum design, you may find it useful to identify aspects of the curriculum that might be inequitable but still have some benefits. For example, I know that the practice of peer writing workshops, which are so common in English classes, has a history of silencing marginalized voices. However, the collaborative aspect of students working together to give each other feedback means that these peer workshops have the potential to be a positive learning and community-building experience.

That is why I wanted to keep the practice of peer writing workshops even though I knew the harm my own graduate workshops had done. To give some context, my graduate writing workshops were critique-heavy and had, at their core, the rule of silence. That basically meant that every week, we would sit in a circle and tear apart the chosen story while the writer was forced to sit silently and take in the critique without the ability to speak back.

For me, a woman of color, that meant fuming in enforced silence while my all-white workshop (mostly men) were emboldened in their racism and sexism by the rule of silence. They gave me feedback such as, "You should consider making your main character white for more universal appeal. She doesn't *really* need to be Asian."

Although I clearly recognized the racism and sexism I experienced in the workshop, that did not keep me from slowly internalizing the belief that there was no place for my stories. My stories did not have universal appeal. Who would want to read stories about Asian American girls and women having adventures, falling in love, and saving the world?

No one, I concluded. And so I quietly gave up writing.

I thought I lacked the grit, toughness, dedication, or talent necessary to be a writer. In other words, I thought the deficiency was in me rather than the machine of traditional workshops that tried to mold me into a template based on white, male, cishet norms. I have since talked to other BIPOC authors who have had similar stories about being silenced in writing workshops—it turns out that mine was a shockingly common experience.

Fortunately, I have been able to come back to writing through mentorship and community, but I still knew I had to change the ways I designed peer writing workshops in my own classes.

I certainly did not want to replicate the inequitable structures and dehumanizing messages of the traditional workshop model onto my own students.

In general, my students tended to struggle with workshops, finding them unhelpful or being unsure of their own ability to provide useful feedback to their peers. Unfortunately, my efforts to make peer workshops a relevant part of the curriculum did not end up making things better. At first, I asked students to write comments directly on the rough drafts just like I would do with their final drafts, and I asked them to use my grading rubric to guide their reviews in the hopes that they could help each other write essays that met the criteria better. Basically, these peer writing workshops were not designed to be multiple, flexible, equitable, or humanizing—and they certainly weren't empowering students to freely express themselves or their creativity.

Redesigning these workshops was a process that took time, reflection, learning from other sources, and collaboration with other people. I will include these sources in the Works Cited at the end of the chapter, but for the purpose of this book, I will just share that I redesigned my workshop to do two main things:

- Center the writer's own questions about their writing rather than preset questions I gave them
- Provide an alternate option to peer writing workshops

After redesigning the peer workshop, I conducted a student survey to see how it was working, and the comments were overwhelmingly positive. Here is what one student said on the survey:

> I feel like most peer workshop groups I have done, feedback was based on helping each other get our papers closer to the teachers expectations. I really like the idea of asking specific questions. In the past I feel like without asking a specific question in regards to feedback, peers would usually just try to help with syntax or grammatical errors. Asking specific questions helped me get much more thoughtful feedback and I think helped me improve my subject matter overall.

I have to admit that I was feeling pretty good about my redesigned peer writing workshop... until Cora came to talk to me after class one day.

Designing Practices through Responsive Relationships

Remember Cora? She was the student from Chapter 2 who talked about "unlearning the script." I was thrilled that Cora was taking me at my word when I encouraged her to let me know if she encountered a structural barrier instead of assuming the problem was with her. This time, the problem was with the peer workshop she had just participated in.

Cora explained that one of her peer group members, a white male student who was generally thoughtful and insightful, had given her feedback to change the direction of her essay. The feedback didn't seem connected to the questions she asked about her essay and didn't make her feel supported in what she wanted to write.

Looking visibly upset, she said, "I'm sure Ron didn't mean anything by it. Maybe I'm overreacting."

"You're not," I assured her at once. I remembered my own graduate writing workshop, and the last thing I wanted was for Cora to think that she wasn't "tough" enough to take feedback and to question herself as a writer... and as a person. "You have every right to feel the way you do," I told her. "You wrote something that was meaningful to you, and it is painful when you're not being heard in the workshop."

Cora took a breath, and I wondered how long she had been holding it. "You're right."

As firmly as I could, I said, "This definitely is not a problem with you or your writing or your ability to take feedback." In this moment, I wanted to counter the messages about how students were supposed to develop resilience and passively take feedback, especially since these messages were so damaging to BIPOC women like Cora.

Cora smiled. "Okay, I hear you." She hastened to add, "I don't mean to criticize Ron. He's usually so great, and I think that's why his comments took me by surprise."

"I get that," I said, "And I agree that Ron is great too. I imagine that he's probably been taught that trying to 'fix' your writing is what he's supposed to do in a peer workshop." A pang hit me when I realized what the issue really was. "This isn't a problem with Ron—it is a problem with the design of the workshop."

It didn't matter that the workshop was working for most students or that I had built in an alternate option for the peer workshop. The point was that the workshop I had designed wasn't working for Cora, and it was replicating the same white-centric norms that had made my own graduate school workshops so harmful even when I had removed some of the inequitable structural barriers like the rule of silence. Apparently, I wasn't done redesigning the peer writing workshop, but that was okay. It was better than okay.

Listening to students and continuing to design practices for equity are exactly how Anti-Oppressive UD works. Designing for freedom is an organic, ongoing process that grows and changes through responsive relationships with students.

For my peer writing workshop, flexible design and multiple options certainly helped this practice be more accessible—but I also needed to acknowledge the inequitable structure of the workshop model. Ron was a kind person, and was also a white male in a society that assumes competence and authority in white men. That meant he had the privilege of having his opinions automatically centered and validated in a writing workshop—unless the workshop was designed to explicitly challenge those inequitable white and male-centered and white and male-dominant norms.

In thinking about how this workshop model was inequitable for Cora, an Indigenous woman writing from her own cultural experiences, histories, and context, I also recalled other incidents that could have informed me that the workshop model was inequitable. MLL (Multiple Language Learners) students, mostly Asian, have told me they didn't feel comfortable giving writing feedback to "native speakers." Their discomfort, I was starting to understand, was due to an assumed dominance and authority in White Mainstream English (Baker-Bell). I realized then that I had to redesign the peer writing workshop so all students could fully and confidently express themselves.

Redesigning the Peer Writing Workshop through Multiplicity

To create anti-oppressive and student-centered workshops, I knew I had to teach students how to interact in culturally responsive and sustaining ways, so I redesigned my curriculum to build in lessons and modeling on making the peer writing workshop equitable and humanizing. In fact, I realized that I could create something completely new—a Peer Support Workshop. I have actually taught the Peer Support Workshop model in writing spaces outside of my own classrooms, and I can say that it has been wonderful to see writers so empowered and supported by this model.

I am happy to say that students in my classrooms have found the Peer Support Workshop model to be just as responsive and sustaining for their own writing. However, since Anti-Oppressive UD is about multiplication rather than subtraction, I *also* kept the original peer writing workshop model that focuses on written feedback to the writer's questions. Of course, I also kept the independent alternate option. These options were working well for some students, and I was aware that the Peer Support Workshop model wouldn't work for everyone—but that is the point. I needed multiple and distinct options that *would* work for everyone.

Adding the Peer Support Workshop model as an option has made it more possible for my students to find the option they need to develop their writing and creative expression. One of my favorite parts of this activity is simply walking around and listening to the rich, supportive discussions all around me. This is a composite narrative of those conversations and, as a bonus, it features Holly!

The Peer Support Workshop in Practice

Holly: "Okay, so I guess I'm going first. My vision for my essay is that I want to challenge the single story of Indigenous communities. That's why I want to write about the theme

	of hope in *Solar Storms*. It's written by Linda Hogan, an Indigenous author—Chickasaw, actually."
Troy:	"That sounds cool."
Kate:	"I remember when you talked about that experience last year when your English teacher said reservations were just places of poverty and alcoholism. Is that why you wanted to write about hope?"
Holly:	"Yes! That's exactly why I want to write this essay. I want readers to see Indigenous communities as places of hope and healing like it is in this novel."
Kate:	"Got it. So, what's your first question?"
Holly:	"Well, I'm struggling with my thesis. I know I want to write about the danger of a single story, but I can't seem to connect this to the idea of environmental justice."
Troy:	"I didn't read *Solar Storms*. What is the environmental justice theme in the book?"
Holly:	"So, in the book, the main character Angel goes on an epic journey with her older female relatives to protest the building of a dam that will destroy the land and their way of life."
Troy:	"That's really interesting! What was it that you said before about Indigenous communities as places of hope? Maybe there's a connection there?"
Holly:	"Oh! Yes, Angel's Indigenous community is a place of hope and healing but also of *resistance*. The awfulness that happens to the community is the effect of white colonialism and the taking and destruction of Indigenous lands. That's totally environmental injustice. But we don't have many stories that talk about that, so people just assume that Indigenous people have all these problems because that's just the way we are, which isn't true at all."
Kate:	"Yeah! That reminds me of something Adichie said in that video about the danger of a single story."
Holly:	"Right! That where you start a story can erase important background. Like Adichie said, you get a whole different story if you start with Indigenous people fighting for their land back than if you start the story with white conquest."

Troy: "So if you were to put this all together…"
Holly: "I would say that *Solar Storms* resists the single story of Indigenous communities being only places of poverty and despair because it shows these communities as places of hope, healing, and resistance to colonialism and environmental injustice that caused these problems in the first place."
Kate: "Wow! I think that's your thesis!"
Troy: "It's a great thesis. I'd read that essay!"
Holly: "Thank you for helping me think that through!"

All Students Can Learn

I want to come back to my core belief that all students can learn if we create curriculum and practices with multiplicity, flexible design, equity, and humanizing pedagogy. However, before we can design with Anti-Oppressive UD principles, we might need to let go of the curriculum and practices that were used to teach us. That was what I needed to do with the peer writing workshop. For a long time, the peer writing workshop model was the air I breathed, and I didn't see anything inequitable about this practice. I imagine there are practices that you might have been taught and that you now use in your own classrooms. It might be worth thinking about whether these practices need to be redesigned.

For example, about the time I was in third or fourth grade, my teacher introduced the multiplication unit. At some point in this unit, we would be divided into two groups: those who could complete a series of timed tests on the multiplication table… and those who couldn't. Naturally, this caused me anxiety even though my father was a math teacher who would often spring math problems over the dinner table. Fortunately for me, I passed the tests—but not everyone did.

The truth is that I had class privilege. My parents weren't working multiple low-paying jobs to make rent and put food on the table, so they had the time and resources to drill me on the multiplication table. As a result of passing the tests, I was put into a group that went to a separate part of the room to do "advanced math" while the other students continued to do multiplication drills. This was an inequitable system that gave advantages to students like me who had economic privilege, and this is an inequity that needed to be acknowledged before changes could be made.

And these changes would not have been hard to make. The students in the other part of the room understood the concept of multiplication just as well as the students doing advanced math—they just couldn't pass the timed multiplication table test. Yet, if the class had been redesigned with multiple options (pun intended) like a times table chart or the choice to do fewer math problems or even a calculator, then *everyone* could have done the "advanced math." In other words, all students can meet learning standards as long as the curriculum and practices are designed with multiplicity, flexible design, equity, and humanizing pedagogy.

On that hopeful note, I want to end the chapter by sharing another question Nicki answered in the student survey. How has Anti-Oppressive UD in classroom *structure, policy, practice, curriculum, assignments*, or *assessments* supported your learning or created equitable access to your education in this class?

Nicki's Survey Response to the Second Question

The actual curriculum of this course was phenomenal. I've only studied academic texts written in non-"academic" styles in a linguistic class before, but to do so in an English course showed me the value of own-voice and diverse writing styles in academia as well as creative writing. The approach to the intercultural aspects of the class also felt incredibly compassionate and considerate. There was an emphasis on learning through understanding (understanding the realities of marginalized people in our society, understanding the systems that create marginalization, etc.) instead of through learning facts and history, which I feel can often lack the empathy necessary for such topics. Overall, this course was absolutely phenomenal, as a person of color it was invaluable to take a course with my experiences so firmly in mind and respected.

Learning through Understanding

I am always incredibly touched when I read Nicki's response. It gives me a sense of hope. That hope comes from the knowledge that curriculum and practices designed for freedom can go a long way in healing the harm that inequitable and dehumanizing curriculum and practices have done. I love what Nicki says about learning through understanding… and respect, and compassion, and consideration. Although these are values that might not appear in state or district learning standards, I believe *these* are the standards we can build into our curriculum and practices.

Chapter 3 Teaching Toolkit Example

I'm going to share just the bare bones of a sample curriculum of a high school English class to focus on the learning outcomes that I shared earlier in the chapter—rewritten to focus on the specific discipline of ELA. Remember that Anti-Oppressive UD is about multiplicity, not subtraction, so the state ELA learning standards will also be met by this curriculum!

I'm including just two units of the class, but to give you an idea of what the year's curriculum would look like, the other units are: "Poetry for Joy and Resistance," "Alternate Pasts, Possible Futures, and Other Worlds," and "Fairy Tale Retellings." Note that I include capstone assessments, which I will be talking about more in Chapter 7 "Creating Equitable Assignments and Assessments" with Anti-Oppressive UD.

My goal is to use the principles of multiplicity, flexible design, equity, and humanizing pedagogy to create a curriculum so that students will be able to meet the following learning goals:

- Understand the multiplicity and importance of diverse representation through reading.
- Demonstrate responsiveness to a multiplicity of cultures, identities, and histories through writing and other forms of expression.
- Express and sustain the student's own cultures, identities, and interests in ways that are meaningful to the student—through writing and other forms of expression.

Sample Curriculum for High School English

I. Rewriting the Rules Unit

Possible Texts

- *Fresh Ink*, edited by Lamar Giles
- *Piecing Me Together* by Renee Watson
- *Hearts Unbroken* by Cynthia Leitich Smith
- *Ace of Spades* by Faridah Àbíké-Íyímídé
- *I'll Be the One* by Lyla Lee
- *Lesbiana's Guide to Catholic School* by Sonora Reyes
- *All You Have to Do* by Autumn Allen
- *Felix Ever After* by Kacen Callender
- *Get a Grip, Vivy Cohen* by Sarah Kapit
- Alternate Choice text

Possible Other Sources

- Rudine Sims Bishop's essay "Mirrors, Windows, Sliding Glass Doors."
- Jason Reynolds' interview "There's Nothing Wrong with Us"

Assessment: Capstone Project

II. Rewriting the Bard's Tale Unit

Possible Texts

- *That Way Madness Lies*, edited by Dahlia Adler
- *Fat Ham* by James Ijames
- *A Thousand Acres* by Jane Smiley
- *These Violent Delights* by Chloe Gong
- *Street Love* by Walter Dean Myers
- *10 Things I Hate about You* movie
- Alternate Choice Text
- The Shakespeare play being rewritten (ie. *Hamlet, Romeo and Juliet, King Lear, Taming of the Shrew*)

Possible Other Sources

- "James Ijames on 'Fat Ham,' the South, and Embodying the Story"
- "These Violent Delights: An Interview with Chloe Gong"

That's a sampling of my curriculum! Again, students aren't expected to read every book in each unit—they choose the book that they're drawn to or talk to me to figure out an alternate choice. And, as you can tell, I have a wide range of themed units that speak to my own interests and are also designed for student choice.

I understand that it might seem tricky to put a curriculum where students are all reading different books into practice. However, I found that it often takes just a slight reframing to make this work. For example, instead of discussing how a common book connects to the theme of rewriting the rules, students might instead discuss the commonalities and differences of how their individual book rewrites the rules. The Peer Support Workshop was also an example of how students can effectively participate in a discussion without all having read the same book.

It is my hope that when you are designing your own curriculum and practices under the principles of multiplicity, flexible design, equity, and humanizing pedagogy, you *and* your students can bring all of yourselves into the classroom.

 **Teacher Toolkit Exercise: Practicing Multiplicity**

It can feel like a lot to use the Anti-Oppressive UD principles of multiplicity, flexible design, equity, and humanizing pedagogy to redesign the entire educational structure of your classes all at once! So, why don't we start slowly? It's important to remember that you don't have to throw everything out. After all, Anti-oppressive UD is about multiplicity, not subtraction. The next chapters will guide you through the design of policies, assignments, and assessments, but for now, I'm going to ask you to focus on designing with multiplicity.

Multiplicity, Part 1

Let's begin with the overall concept of multiplicity and choose just **one** aspect of your classroom that you could add options to. Maybe it is a due date extension option, an alternative reading, another way to present material, more assignment options, or an alternate way to take a quiz, or... you get the idea!

- **Prompt**: What is one activity, assignment, or assessment that you can add more options to?
- **Directions**: Take some time to either list your ideas or write about how to make an activity, assignment, or assessment more equitable and accessible with multiple options. Once you finish, your teacher toolkit will contain a redesigned activity, assignment, or assessment with multiplicity.

Multiplicity, Part 2

Multiplicity is not only about creating more options in activities, assignments, and assessments—it is also about the multiplicity of diverse representation to resist and counter the dangers of a single story. Even adding an example of a BIPOC scientist or an LGBTQ+ mathematician or a disabilities activist in your curriculum is helpful in creating a humanizing curriculum where students can see themselves reflected and understand other identities and cultures in their richness and fullness.

- ◆ **Prompt**: What is a text or example of diverse representation that you can add to your curriculum?
- ◆ **Directions**: Take some time to either list your ideas or write about how to make your curriculum more humanizing with diverse representation. Once you finish, your teacher toolkit will contain a redesigned curriculum with a multiplicity of diverse representation.

What This Tool Is for: You can use this tool to create equitable teaching practices and a humanizing curriculum through multiplicity.

Works Cited

Adichie, Chimamanda. "The Danger of a Single Story." *Youtube*, uploaded by *TED Talk*, 10 March, 2014. Accessed 7 June 2023. https://www.youtube.com/watch?v=D9Ihs241zeg

Bishop, Rudine Sims. "Mirrors, Windows, Sliding Glass Doors." *Reading Is Fundamental*, Scenic Regional Library, Aug. 2017, scenicregional.org/wp-content/uploads/2017/08/Mirrors-Windows-and-Sliding-Glass-Doors.pdf. Accessed 2 Aug. 2024.

Chavez, Felicia Rose. *The Anti-Racist Writing Workshop: How to Decolonize the Creative Writing Classroom*. Haymarket Books, 2021.

"Common Core State Standards for English Language Arts and Literacy in History/Social Studies, Science, and Technical Studies." PDF. *Washington Office of Superintendent of Public Instruction*, 2011, ospi.k12.wa.us/student-success/resources-subject-area/english-language-arts/english-language-arts-learning-standards. Accessed 22 Oct. 2024.

Gay, Geneva. "Preparing for Culturally Responsive Teaching." *Sage Journals*, vol. 53, no. 2, Mar. 2002, pp. 106–116, journals.sagepub.com/doi/10.1177/0022487102053002003. Accessed 22 July 2023.

Gong, Chloe, interviewed by Dani Hedlund. "*These Violent Delights*: An Interview with Chloe Gong." *F(r)iction*, http://frictionlit.org/these-violent-delights-an-interview-with-chloe-gong/?srsltid=AfmBOooH0scBigCuWUkxd2emk3hJZDDDFGoK7qWwOFgRqkRrublEGMj. Accessed 15 Aug. 2024.

Hogan, Linda. *Solar Storms*. Scribner, 1997.

Ijames, James. "James Ijames on 'Fat Ham,' the South, and Embodying the Story." *Interviewed by Jessica Bedford. Southern Review of Books*, 4 May 2021, http://southernreviewofbooks.com/2021/05/04/fat-ham-james-ijames-interview. Accessed 23 Oct. 2024.

Ma, Diana. "Teaching Diverse Books." Dianamaauthor.com, 11 Nov. 2022, https://dianamaauthor.com/teaching-diverse-books/. Accessed 18 Nov. 2024.

Ma, Diana. "Why I Hope Readers See Themselves in My YA Chinese-American Protagonists." Guest Blog. *We Need Diverse Books*. https://diversebooks.org/why-i-hope-readers-see-themselves-in-my-chinese-american-ya-protagonist/. 2020, Dec. 1. Accessed 16 July 2024.

Ma, Diana, and Christina Scheuer. "How We Developed Our Collaborative Feedback Process." *Highlights Foundation*, 18 Jan. 2023, www.highlightsfoundation.org/2023/01/18/how-we-developed-our-collaborative-feedback-process/. Accessed 23 Oct. 2024.

Muhammad, Gholdy. *Cultivating Genius. An Equity Framework for Culturally and Historically Responsive Literacy*. Scholastic, 2020.

Paris, Django, and H. Samy Alim. "What Is Culturally Sustaining Pedagogy and Why Does It Matter?" *Culturally Sustaining Pedagogies: Teaching and Learning for Justice in a Changing World*, edited by Paris and Alim, Teachers College Press, 2017, pp. 1–21.

Reynolds, Jason. "'There's Nothing Wrong with Us'—Jason Reynolds Says Normalizing Anxiety Is A Way To Beat It." Interviewed by Stephen Colbert. *YouTube*, uploaded by *The Late Show with Stephen Colbert*, 2 Dec. 2021, www.youtube.com/watch?v=nNzYE_4DdtA. Accessed 23 Oct. 2024.

Salesses, Matthew. *Craft in the Real World: Rethinking Fiction Writing and Workshopping*. Catapult Books, 2021.

4

Building Equitable Classroom Policies with Anti-Oppressive Universal Design

When I started teaching with an Anti-Oppressive Universal Design (UD) framework, one of the first things I changed was my classroom policies. Many of my original policies were simply copied and pasted from the template given out by my school or echoed the wording of the school policies. The problem with these standard policies is they are created to uphold the status quo and are not intended to understand distinct structural oppression and dismantle inequitable barriers.

In other words, many of my original class policies were not tools of equity. In fact, these classroom policies kept my students from having full access to their learning. Fortunately, Anti-Oppressive UD gave me a framework to create policies that supported and empowered students instead of ones that restricted students' freedom to learn and to feel supported in expressing their full authentic selves.

Designing equitable class policies is more than revising the wording of standard, inequitable policies. It is about redesigning the structure of my class with the Anti-Oppressive UD principles of multiplicity, flexible design, equity, and humanizing pedagogy.

In this chapter I will talk about how I used Anti-Oppressive UD to redesign the following two classroom policies:

- Attendance Policy
- Late Assignment Policy

The Role of the Teacher in Equitable Design

I have always taught with a social justice mindset when it came to the content of my classes and my relationships with my students. However, when it came to classroom policies, I often defaulted to the standard policies and wording of my department or my school. If I thought about it at all, I probably assumed that there was nothing I could do about the larger policies of my school or that classroom policies were less important, logistical aspects of my teaching that I did not need to address with an equity lens. I was, of course, wrong.

We might have little control over school structures and policies, but what we do in the classroom makes all the difference in our students' lives. I don't think I fully realized this simple truth until I conducted a survey to ask students what helped them be successful in their K-12 school experiences. I was expecting that students would talk about big school policies around equity, fair grading practices, or engaging assignments, and, yes, there certainly was a lot of that. But overwhelmingly, students shared that it was the act of a teacher reaching out, expressing care, giving encouragement, or checking in that was the most impactful.

I want to share a student experience to illustrate that it isn't always the school-wide policies or supports that are the most helpful to students, but rather the individual efforts of teachers. This experience is from a student narrative, shared with her permission and with the use of a pseudonym.

Val's Story

In high school, Val would often make herself go to school at the expense of her mental health. As she put it,

> School only allowed a certain amount of unexcused absences before something permanent would go on my record, or worse, I might have to repeat the year. But crying uncontrollably wasn't an illness and excused absences only came with a call from being sick or a doctor's note.

Val felt that school-wide initiatives like mental health awareness month "were like putting a leaf on top of sand: they were surface-level inclusion tactics that almost always floated away or sank below the radar." She went on to say,

> The school did one little, sappy powerpoint about how it's normal to feel your body changing and to reach out when times were tough, then they wrapped it up, turned on the lights and it was like the whole discussion had been tossed into the corner like me. I didn't understand why more people didn't feel like this. Was it me? Was I cracked inside, my emotions spilling through the void that everyone else had shut? No one else was wilted or sad, so I pretend I wasn't either.

What ended up helping Val the most was one of her teachers telling her, "You know, you could always call and say you are sick when days like this come up. I know the school's policy can be rigid, but you shouldn't force yourself to come."

With her teacher's encouragement, Val worked out a strategy where she would call in sick and take care of her mental health with her mother's support. She made up her work and kept up her grades and managed to successfully complete school. This is what Val said about the experience: "It made me realize how school may not adapt to me but I could adapt to it by taking the time I needed for myself."

Designing Equitable Classroom Policies to Counter Inequitable School Policies

A Leaf on Top of Sand—that is one of the phrases that stays with me from Val's moving narrative. It perfectly encapsulates why "one size fits all" initiatives like mental health awareness month are not always as helpful as we might hope they will be. Adding a generic presentation to a class in order to address mental health is like putting a leaf on a vast expanse of shifting sand—not at all useful or specific to the situation. Again, we need the multiplicity, flexibility, equity, and humanizing pedagogy of Anti-Oppressive UD to design intentionally and specifically for freedom.

It took Val's teacher and mother working together to work around a rigid attendance policy that led to her finally getting the support she needed, which did not come in the form of official support from the school. Val's teacher may not have been consciously teaching under an Anti-Oppressive UD framework, but she interacted with Val in humanizing ways, prioritizing her individual needs rather than the rigid policies of the school. This ended up being extremely helpful for Val.

Another thing that strikes me, however, is the last sentence in Val's excerpt: "It made me realize how school may not adapt to me but I could adapt to it."

Val shouldn't have had to adapt to the structure of her school. Too often, students are required to adapt to inequitable structures. It would make a whole lot more sense for our structures, policies, and practices to adapt to *them*. This is exactly the kind of adaptability we can design in the classroom. And that includes classroom policies.

In fact, we have a responsibility to make our classroom policies multiple, flexible, equitable, and humanizing to counter the conformist, rigid, inequitable, and dehumanizing effects of many school-wide policies.

I'd like to share another student story that shows how larger school policies can negatively impact students and why we need to design equitable policies in the classroom. This student response is from Nicki, whom we met in Chapter 3, "Building Equitable Curriculum and Practices with Anti-Oppressive Universal Design." In that chapter, I shared Nicki's survey response where she talked about problems with curriculum and practices in the classroom. This is actually the first part of her response where she is talking about the problems of larger school policy. Again, her response is from a survey I conducted at the end of a class that specifically discussed both the reality of and resistance to oppressive educational structures.

Nicki's response below is to the following question: "How did classroom *structure*, *policy*, teaching *practice*, *curriculum*, *assignments*, or *assessments* create a barrier in your learning or access to education in your K-12 experience (especially in middle school or high school)?"

Nicki's Survey Response

My high school had an inflexible attendance policy that primarily targeted the POC [People of Color]/lower-income students. Being tardy to school resulted in a 15-minute detention, and six tardies a quarter led to a full hour detention. Many of the POC/lower-income students at my high school lived outside of the city (like myself) and had a 45- to 60-minute commute in the mornings that often involved traffic, so it was primarily those students who would be late. For me, it meant having to wake up 3 hours before school started (5 a.m.) just to make sure I got there on time.

The Cost of Inflexibility

Nicki's story is just as devastating as Val's, and both stories show the damage done by inequitable attendance policies. At Nicki's school, student tardiness was seen as a deficit to be "fixed" with a punitive and "inflexible attendance policy" that used detention as a solution rather than addressing the actual inequitable barriers that students of color and lower-income students faced. It is absolutely inequitable to expect a population of primarily students of color and lower-income students to get up earlier and commute longer than their white and wealthier peers. And it is an egregious harm to punish students if they do not meet this inequitable expectation.

To be clear, the cost of inflexible, deficit-model policies is not *just* that students have to get up at 5 a.m. to get to school on time (although that is bad enough). The cost is that students, particularly marginalized students, are failing because schools are not addressing the root systemic causes of racism, economic injustice, and ableism with their policies. Instead, school policies often uphold systems of power and privilege. This, obviously, is not conducive to equity.

The National Center for Education Statistics (NCES) 2019-2020 Report shows that disabled students graduate high school at 70.6% compared with the overall average graduation rate of 86.5%. English learners graduate at a rate of 71.3%, and "economically disadvantaged students" graduate at a rate of 81.3%. Black students graduate at a rate of 81.1% compared with white students at 90.2%.

Looking at the NCES numbers, I see that schools have a serious problem with systemic ableism, racism, and economic injustice, and this problem cannot be fixed with inflexible and punitive school policies like the policy of detention for tardies. I want to emphasize that these policies harm *all* students, but it is students of color, lower-income students, disabled students, and English language learners who pay disproportionately high costs.

Nicki's story is a powerful reminder of why it is important to teach with justice and equity. As I said before, individual teachers can't change a school-wide attendance policy, but we *can* design a multiple, flexible, equitable, and humanizing classroom policy to counter the conformity, rigidity, inequity, and dehumanization of a larger school policy. In my case, that meant looking at my original attendance policy and redesigning it.

Redesigning My Attendance Policy

A good place to start in redesigning rigid attendance policies is to avoid language that touts the importance of regular attendance as the *only* path to educational success. This kind of language completely disregards the structural barriers that could prevent disabled, low-income, BIPOC (Black, Indigenous, and People of Color), and other marginalized students from regularly attending school. A punitive and inflexible attendance policy created unjust hardships for both Nicki and Val, and exhortations about the importance of regular attendance would not have helped either student. In fact, pretending that all students have the equal opportunity to attend school would ignore the very real structural oppression that might prevent students from attending.

What we can do, however, is design a classroom attendance policy that provides clear, equitable, accessible, and flexible ways for students to keep up with the class work. One of those ways can be through regular attendance, but if that is the *only* way, then our classroom policy becomes rigid and inequitable.

Here's an example of an attendance policy that contains the kind of inflexible language I've used in the past.

Standard Attendance Policy
Regular and punctual attendance is vital to your success in school, so please make every effort to attend class on time. Missing class will negatively affect your learning. [Insert reminder of whatever consequences the school has set up for absences and tardies.] Communication is also important, so if you must miss class for an excused absence, please discuss your circumstances with me as soon as possible. Also, if you miss class, it is your responsibility to meet with me to get caught up.

What Makes This an Inequitable Attendance Policy?

On the surface, the above attendance policy might seem like a perfectly reasonable one. I must have thought so since I've used one like it in the past. It's true that there's nothing that's overtly draconian or authoritarian in its wording, but if I put myself in Val's and Nicki's place, I can see the damaging assumptions in the wording.

For example, there's the language of "make every effort to attend class on time." This implies that if students don't attend class on time, then it must be due to a lack of effort. Yet, Val's narrative describes how she pushed herself through unimaginable pain over and over again to be physically present in a classroom where she desperately tried to hold herself together. Her absences were certainly not due to a lack of effort.

Too often, I hear the harmful refrain that students will be successful if we simply create firm expectations and build up the grit or perseverance to meet our expectations. Schools often include growth mindset units to increase students' ability to persist. I actually attended a long workshop where the focus was on using the productive persistence model to help students with attendance. The problem with productive persistence when it comes to attendance (or anything else) is that it, again, focuses on "fixing" students rather than an inequitable system.

Including wording in the classroom policy that echoes the expectations and consequences a school sets is also likely to reinforce the harm of that larger policy. For example, Val was so concerned with a mark on her permanent record or repeating a year that she put all her energy to attend school to the detriment of her learning and her mental health. In other words, Val's school attendance policy did exactly what it was intended to do—it set an expectation of attendance and implied that there was something wrong with the student if they didn't attend. That's how Val felt until her teacher called out the school attendance policy as "rigid."

This critique of the system might seem minor (after all, it's not like her teacher could change that larger system). However, this small acknowledgement empowered Val to resist an oppressive attendance policy and find a way to work around the system.

My old attendance policy did not empower students. It simply echoed the traditional educational assumptions of student deficits and reinforced the existing oppressive system. What I needed was an acknowledgement that inequitable barriers to attendance *do* exist. Without such an acknowledgement, I risked perpetuating a damaging narrative that if a student is unsuccessful in my class due to absences, then it must be because of some inherent deficit in the student rather than the fault of my class design.

Another major flaw in my old attendance policy is that I was putting the responsibility to "get caught up" on the student rather than creating a clear system that would allow them an alternative to in-person class time to get caught up. I needed to recognize the problem of standardized language and assumptions in my attendance policy and stop trying to change student behaviors. To be clear, it was *not* absences that caused students to be unsuccessful in my classes. It was my failure to design a flexible and equitable system for students to complete their work in multiple ways.

Not incidentally, my old attendance policy was an unsustainable system for *me*. I was constantly meeting with students who were absent and trying to replicate the class content and activities in individual tutoring sessions that were overwhelming for both me and my student. But what was the alternative? The students who were absent didn't want to miss crucial class content and activities, and I didn't want them to fall behind and get discouraged about school either. We were stuck in an inequitable and unsustainable system, but neither I or my students could see a way out. It was no wonder I was so fixated on stressing the importance of regular attendance even though a part of me was uneasy with this insistence. Was I trying to "fix" my students? Was I the oppressor in the oppressive teacher-student relationship that Paulo Freire criticized?

Yes, actually. I was.

No system of punishment (marks on a permanent record, detention, or forcing students to repeat a year) or rewards (certificate of attendance, pizza party, or ice cream vouchers) would address the inequities that keep students from attending school or create a situation where students would magically come to class everyday.

Yet, I had a real problem in my classes with students missing crucial course content and falling behind. Unfortunately, I didn't know what to do about it without falling into an oppressor-oppressed dynamic and treating my students as if they were objects to be fixed. My default position was to throw up my hands and exclaim, "The school attendance policy is punitive and ineffective, but how do I get students to attend regularly?"

It was, of course, the wrong focus.

I didn't need to spend my time and energy on trying to get my students to attend class, and my students certainly didn't need threats against their permanent record or promises of perfect attendance awards.

What I needed was a more sustainable system, and what my students needed was an equitable system that allowed them agency over their education. Fortunately, our needs were aligned. What we needed was a policy redesigned under the Anti-Oppressive UD framework.

My Redesigned Attendance Policy

Again, the Anti-Oppressive UD principles of *Multiplicity, Flexible Design, Equity, and Humanizing Pedagogy* were the principles I kept in mind when I redesigned my attendance policy. As with all the samples in this book, please keep in mind that I'm sharing these policies, not as templates, but as examples. You might come up with something different with the principles of the Anti-Oppressive UD framework, and that's just fine! Here is my redesigned policy:

Flexible Attendance Policy

I recognize that structural barriers may prevent you from attending class. If you need to miss class, please find the make-up work in the module item titled "Class Material" for that day in the class management system.

I have designed class supports for you to access the class materials and ask that you follow this process if you miss a class. These class materials might also be helpful for those of you who attended class since they are a great way to review the content we covered in class.

1. *Carefully review the "Class Materials" in the online course modules for the day you are absent. These modules may include lecture notes, videos shown in class, supplemental readings, and so on.*
2. *Make sure that you submit the "Writing Reflection on Class Materials" that corresponds to each class session. This will give you the chance to reflect on and learn the class materials*

in an alternative way to doing the in-class activities (those who attend the in-class session get an automatic opt-out from submitting that day's Writing Reflection on Class Materials online).
3. After reviewing all class materials, assignments, and doing all the required readings, please reach out to me with specific questions you might have. I find that specific questions result in more useful responses. I understand the impulse to ask a general question like "What did I miss?" However, it can be hard for me to provide a focused response to a general question, so I'm likely to point you to the "Class materials" module item that covers the overall content of that day's class. Here's an example of a specific question that might be more useful to you: "In the essay assignment you asked us to preview, you said that we need at least one secondary source and listed some options. I was hoping to use _____ instead. Would that work as a secondary source?"

What Makes This an Equitable Attendance Policy?

With this policy, I am no longer focused on getting students to attend or making value judgments if they don't. I am not reminding them of the consequences they face for absences under the school attendance policy. They know it already, and I do not want to reinforce the message that they are deserving of punishment or that there is something inherently wrong with them if they can't "make every effort" to attend class.

Instead, I have acknowledged the barriers that keep students from attending class and redesigned my class structure so that it has *multiple* and *flexible* options for students to learn the course content and does not rely on in-person attendance alone. Now if a student misses class, they have a transparent process to access and learn the content so they don't fall behind. I have designed this structure with *equity* and *humanizing pedagogy* principles to counter inequitable structural barriers, to decenter my authority as the keeper of all knowledge, and to empower students to have agency in their learning.

This redesign benefits *everyone*, not only the students who miss class and need an alternate way to learn. Students who attend class but find it helpful to review the content can also easily access the daily class materials with this redesigned structure. There's yet another benefit of this system. Since implementing this more flexible, equitable system, I've been able to significantly reduce student workload without compromising student learning.

The reason for this is simple. If I teach under the traditional educational model of conformity (equality rather than equity), then I am teaching under a system that requires all students to do the same thing at the same time. This inevitably results in duplication of work (not the kind of multiplicity I'm advocating for).

Under my old system, for example, I used to require two written Reading Responses a week to be turned in online. These would consist of a couple of paragraphs and would be given points for completion. I would do a quick scan to see if they more or less did what the prompt asked for and then give full credit. I didn't expect that these responses would take too long to complete, but a few of my students were struggling to keep up with these Reading Responses.

It wasn't until I had a conversation with one of these students that I realized what the problem was. I offered advice to my student along the lines of "Don't overthink it and don't spend too much time on it. I'll give you full credit if you just turn something in. We basically did the same thing in class, so just pull from the class activity/group work/discussion to do your response."

That's when my student asked, "If we basically did the same thing in class, then why do we need to submit a Reading Response online?"

His question pulled me up short. Why was I asking students to submit a Reading Response online? Actually, I had an answer once I thought about it. My reason was that the Reading Response assignments weren't actually for the students who were in class. They were for the absent students who didn't get the opportunity to learn from the class activity/group work discussion. The students who were in class didn't need the Reading Response assignment to learn the concept or content, so I was doubling their workload for no good reason except I felt I had to treat the students equally by giving everyone the same assignments regardless of what they actually needed. That is not equity.

Once I realized this, I knew I had to redesign my class structure with the equity, flexible design, multiplicity, sustainability, and humanizing pedagogy principles of Anti-Oppressive UD. That is how the multiple options of my Flexible Attendance policy came into being. By giving students who attended class an automatic opt-out on the daily Writing Reflections on Class Materials, I was giving them credit and acknowledging their work and learning in class. That way, I could remove the Reading Response assignment, reducing students' workload without affecting the outcomes of the class.

However, I needed to give students who missed class an option too, and it couldn't simply be completing the Reading Response because that was designed as a "one size fits all" assignment (a general response to whatever reading we happened to be doing). This Reading Response was supposed to meet the needs of the students who attended class and the students who were absent—but it ended up meeting *no one's* needs (as often happens with "one size fits all" models). However, since I intended the Writing Reflection on Class Materials to be an option for students who missed the learning done in class, I could design it to meet this specific need.

As you can see, when I redesigned my attendance policy, I wasn't just revising wording—I was dismantling and rebuilding the entire structure of my class to be multiple, flexible, equitable, and humanizing.

A Sustainable Attendance Policy

I imagine what you might be thinking: "Okay, I can see that this flexible attendance policy might be helpful for students and reduce their workload, but what about *my* workload? Isn't this a lot of extra work?"

I have two responses. First, this is just *one* example of a redesigned policy, and it might not work for you. Again, that's okay.

You can use Anti-Oppressive UD to design a different system that is sustainable for you.

Second, this system ended up being a lot less work for me and made my teaching more sustainable. Let me explain how, and this isn't meant to persuade you or be an argument for why you need to do it this way because there are many paths to designing equitable education!

For one thing, this flexible attendance system cut down on my last-minute frantic attempts to get all my students individually caught up when they were absent. I can't tell you the sense of calm I feel when a student tells me they are going to be absent and then follows it up with, "So, I can just read the Class Materials and do the Writing Reflection for that day, right?"

"Right," I would respond. "Let me know if you have any questions!"

And that's it. No figuring out what they would miss or giving a twenty-minute impromptu tutoring session on that day's lesson or emailing links and assignments or showing them where to find materials in the online class management system. It was all already there. The calm comes from the knowledge that I have provided students with a clear transparent process that does not require extra work on my part.

I want to come back to Val, who talked about her experience at the start of the chapter. It's true that when Val was taking my class, she was sometimes absent. However, owing to the flexible structure of the class, I didn't need to reteach the content she missed when she was absent, and she was also able to access all the class material independently. Not only did my flexible attendance policy save me time and energy, but it also meant that Val never fell behind. She was able to come back to class, fully caught up and ready to learn—which she *did* very successfully.

It's true that there's more work on the front end to put all the class materials in a module in the online classroom management system for each day and then write a prompt for the writing reflection, but this system resulted in a clearer organizational strategy for my teaching, which meant it was a time saver for me.

Putting the class materials in the online management system became my way of lesson planning. When it came time to teach class, I had all my video links, daily schedule, examples, and discussion prompts all in one place—the daily Class Materials module. All the supplemental material was there too if students wanted them.

As for creating the prompt for daily Writing Reflection for absent students, that was simply a matter of writing prompts based on what we did in class. If there was a discussion, I'd turn the discussion prompt into a writing reflection prompt. If we did a writing exercise, I'd just use the writing exercise prompt. If I lectured on rhetorical appeals, I'd ask them to reflect on a supplemental document on rhetorical appeals that I put in the Class Materials module.

This system also does not increase my grading load because the Writing Reflections are not evaluative. Since the Writing Reflections are meant to be an alternative to learning the material in class, I do not give them evaluative grades. The Writing Reflections are graded simply on completion. Just as I don't grade on the purely subjective quality of classroom participation, I do not grade on the quality of the Writing Reflections. They are meant as a way for students to learn the course content—not for me to evaluate their learning.

I have to admit, however, that none of these sustainable teacher benefits was by design. I suspected that this policy would make my life easier, but I did not deliberately create a policy that would make my teaching sustainable. In Chapter Six, I will talk about purposefully creating policies to be both equitable *and* sustainable (and how these two principles are intertwined), but for this attendance policy redesign, I simply wanted to create an equitable way for my students to learn.

Redesigning an Inequitable Late Assignment Policy

As I said before, my original attendance policy was inequitable in its reinforcement of the status quo, but it was not (overtly at least) punitive. The same could not be said of my original Late Assignment Policy. I'm tempted to add some qualifiers before

I share this punitive and inequitable policy, but I think I'll just put it here before we discuss it further. Okay... ripping off the bandaid!

Late Assignment Policy
Late essays will be deducted 5% for each class day it is late for a maximum of a 10% deduction. Any essay turned in after the beginning of class will be considered late and deducted 5%. After one week past the due date, I will no longer accept late essays. No other assignments will be accepted late. Naturally, if a documented emergency keeps you from turning in an essay on time, we can discuss your circumstances. I will determine what constitutes an emergency, but emergencies, by my definition, do not mean computer problems, jobs, writer's block, and so on.

What Makes This an Inequitable Late Work Policy?

I think it's obvious why this policy is inequitable. Just re-reading it makes me cringe. First of all, the phrase "I will determine what constitutes an emergency" sets me up as an authority figure in the classroom with all the power. Who was I to define what an emergency was?

In order to redesign this policy, however, I had to understand how my own privilege and oppression went into crafting it. Analyzing my policy through an anti-oppressive lens made me see how my class privilege shaped the entitled way I listed computer problems and jobs as things I didn't define as emergencies. Of course, some of my students didn't have computer access or needed to prioritize jobs over their schoolwork. It was my class privilege that gave me computer access as a student and allowed me to see an afterschool job as a means to earn spending money rather than a matter of necessary income. I had to recognize that class privilege before I could take out the oppressive content from my late work policy. I also had to recognize my ableism in listing "writer's block" as another thing I did not consider an emergency.

However, I also needed to understand how my own experience with systemic racism and sexism went into the crafting of my late work policy. As a young Asian American woman, I soon became aware that my authority in the classroom was instantly questioned. I started my first year of teaching high school by telling my students to "Call me Diana!" and a determination to de-center my authority. That did not go well. Teachers with white male privilege might get away with being called by their first names, but my legitimacy as an Asian American woman teacher was challenged at once. The fact that I taught English, a subject some assumed I could not even speak, made it even worse.

I realized that it was not easy to de-center my authority when legitimacy did not look like *me*. I was starting to get written up for my failures in "classroom management and discipline," which terrified me and engulfed me in shame. I was afraid of losing my job.

Without the legitimacy that whiteness or maleness automatically conferred, I felt I had to find another way to establish my authority. I never had a stern or commanding presence and didn't know how to act in a way so unnatural to me. My mentors suggested that I set strict policies. "Students like structure," I was told, and I fell upon this solution with relief. At the time, I did not see that I was trying to approximate white authority (the only model I had) or that structure is not synonymous with rigidity. I was desperate to keep my job and could not have adopted a solution that I consciously knew was white-centered, rigid, and authoritarian.

I told myself that I could let my policies establish my authority and still interact with my students in a responsive and respectful manner. And actually, this solution seemed to work. I thought I was being firm but gentle in enforcing my classroom policies while still establishing a communicative and supportive environment.

Of course, it was a lie I was telling myself.

To resolve the cognitive dissonance of seeing myself as an anti-oppressive teacher and also perpetuating oppressive policies, I had to think of my policies as separate from myself (even though I had created them). I disassociated myself from these policies and thought of them as value-neutral structures I was merely enforcing. I even told students I couldn't make exceptions because it wouldn't be "fair," basing my policies on equality instead of equity even though I was fully aware of the difference in general.

In other words, I had to understand how both privilege and oppression went into my Late Work policy before I could undo the economic injustice, ableism, racism, and sexism that went into my creation of the policy. This recognition did not happen quickly or easily. At some point, I did recognize the egregious inequity in my Late Work policy and took out the last sentence about what I considered to be an emergency, but most of the policy stayed the same for longer than I care to admit. One reason is that I was constantly reminded of why I felt I had to defend my position as an Asian American English teacher in the first place.

For example, one student actually told me he was relieved my English was understandable. What made this incident so painful was that this was an Asian student. He had so internalized the message that the only acceptable English was White Mainstream English and the only acceptable teachers of English were non-Asians. Another student, this time white, told me she had a "bad" experience with another Asian teacher and would have had a "negative impression" of Asian teachers if she hadn't had a positive experience with me.

It astounds me that she thought she was complimenting me, but being told I'm an exception is not a compliment. It is racism. The implication was that she accepted me because I was like her—I was almost white. Unfortunately, this is a backhanded compliment I have heard more than once. And like my Asian student who had internalized the message that only a non-Asian teacher could effectively teach him English, I had unconsciously internalized the message that I had to approximate white norms and authority to be accepted.

In other words, I had to unlearn these internal scripts (as my student Cora would say) in order to redesign my Late Work policy. Again, this did not happen all at once, and my policy went through some revisions that made it less punitive and more inclusive but still did not challenge the overall structural oppression and have the flexibility that would make it an Anti-Oppressive UD policy. Here's an example of a revision that got me closer:

Late Assignment Policy

The important thing to keep in mind is open and respectful communication. I understand that life circumstances can get in the way of school, so if you need to request an extension on an assignment, please email me as soon as possible and before the original due date with a respectful and appropriate request for an extension and an explanation of why you need the extension with the full understanding that it is up to the instructor to decide whether or not to grant an extension. I don't require you to share personal details that you don't feel comfortable revealing, but I'm more likely to grant an extension if I have at least a general idea of why you need one.

Why This Is Still an Inequitable Late Work Policy

As I had said, this is less punitive and more inclusive—but that does not make it an equitable policy. When I look at this version now, it is interesting to me that "the instructor" is in third person when everything else is in first person. I wonder if I was subconsciously distancing myself from the position of authority I was establishing in this statement that it was up to me "to decide whether or not to grant an extension." However, regardless of whether I owned up to my authority or not, this was still a policy that created an inequitable power dynamic in the classroom.

I was framing extensions as something I had the power to give and that students are expected to be grateful to receive as if extensions were some kind of charity. Paulo Freire calls this "False generosity" (44), which "constrains the fearful and subdued, 'the rejects of life,' to extend their trembling hands" (45). Even though I was not aware of it at the time, I was creating an oppressive relationship with my Late Work policy. But how could I, an educator committed to social justice, have ever thought that such a policy was acceptable?

The answer lies in the conformist molds that the machinery of traditional education creates. I believed that I had to encourage "good" work habits and "appropriate" behavior in my students so they would be successful in school and beyond. In fact, I hear other teachers justifying similar late work policies by saying something like, "When students get out into the workforce, they won't be able to turn in their work late. We have to prepare them for the real world!"

My friend and colleague Cathryn Cabral has the perfect response to this argument. As she says, "I don't want to pre-emptively traumatize my students with harsh policies to prepare them for future trauma." I can't improve on Cathryn's response, but I will add that some employees *can* turn in their work past the original deadline and this is often dependent on the type of work they do, which brings up class privilege again.

Speaking of privilege (or lack thereof), even when I revised my original punitive late policy to a more open extension policy, some students, in particular disabled and BIPOC students, would never ask for an extension. I noticed that it was often students with class, white, male cishet, and nondisabled privilege who feel that they have the right to ask for an extension. Of course, these students *should* have the right to ask for an extension. The problem is that this version of my policy does not empower students with marginalized identities to feel they have the same right. Many with marginalized identities have learned that there is something wrong with them if they ask for an extension. That was true for me, and I never felt I could ask for an extension in school. That lesson carried over to the "real world," and it's taken me years to even begin unlearning the internal script that tells me I'm lazy and incompetent for needing an extension.

This version of the Late Work policy did nothing to help students like me to unlearn that internal script. In other words, it does nothing to dismantle the systems of oppression and is, therefore, still an inequitable policy despite its more inclusive language.

That's why I redesigned my Late Policy with the Anti-Oppressive UD principles of multiplicity, flexibility, equity, and humanizing pedagogy. The first thing I did was change it from a "Late Policy" to an "Extension Policy."

My Redesigned Extension Policy

Extension Policy

I understand that there are many circumstances that can prevent you from submitting work by the due date. Therefore, I have created an extension policy to acknowledge the structural barriers that keep students from submitting work by the due date. Please do not hesitate to send me a message through Canvas to request an extension if you need it.

I will do my best to honor all extension requests, and there is no need to feel embarrassed about making this request. Note that I do not ask you to explain the reason you need the extension in your request. I find that the act of explaining the reason for an extension can stop a student from making the request in the first place, so I do not require an explanation. With that said, I am also completely willing to listen and be empathetic if you choose to share why you need an extension. Just know that you don't have to try to convince me since I will make extensions with no judgment as to whether or not your reason is "valid."

What Makes This an Equitable Extension Policy

For one thing, this revised policy does not require students to convince me of their right to an extension, depending on my subjective determination of whether their reason is "valid." I designed the policy under the principle of *humanizing pedagogy* to challenge the classroom oppressor-oppressed classroom power dynamic that "constrains the fearful and subdued, 'the rejects of life,' to extend their trembling hands" (Freire 45) in order to receive an extension. This system dehumanizes students and teachers both because it reduces us to cog in the machine of traditional education.

I am not trying to use the policy to teach students accountability, responsibility, and "respectful and appropriate" behaviors because I am not assuming there is anything lacking in students that keeps them from submitting their work by the due date. Instead, I am acknowledging the "structural barriers." That is why I have changed my "one-size fits all" due date that I used to enforce in the name of fairness and equality. Instead, I have redesigned my policy and my class structure to have options for *multiple* and *flexible* due dates as an explicitly *equitable* policy.

An extension policy created under the principles of multiplicity, flexible design, equity, and humanizing pedagogy challenges the status quo where only those with entitlement determined by class, white, male cishet, and nondisabled privilege feel that they can ask for an extension. I certainly don't want to send that message to my students through my rigid and punitive policies.

I don't see it as my job to create compliant workers who conform without question to oppressive systems. My job as a teacher is to empower students to assert their full humanity, and this purpose is *not* at odds with preparing students for their futures. Yes, the "real world" is hierarchical, punitive, and oppressive. That is why I don't want to teach my students to be a cog in the dehumanizing machine of the real world. Rather, I want to empower my students to *change* that world.

I believe that's what education should be, and what it *can* be when designed with the Anti-Oppressive UD principles of multiplicity, flexible design, equity, and humanizing pedagogy.

I also want to say again that this is not the *only* model of an equitable extension policy. For example, I have a colleague that has all assignments due on the last day of the quarter. That works for her, but it doesn't work for me—and that's fine. Like the attendance policy, the extension policy has to be one that works for you as the teacher.

However, unlike my Flexible Attendance Policy, which was inherently sustainable and did not require additional design elements to make it work for me, my extension policy needed some work to make it sustainable. In Chapter Six "Building Sustainable Teaching with Anti-Oppressive Universal Design," I'll talk about how I did that.

For now, I'd like to share student responses to the flexible attendance and extension policies. These are responses to a survey that asked students to reflect on classroom design that they found helpful. The two elements that students identified as most helpful were the Flexible Attendance and the Extension Policies.

Student Responses about Flexible Attendance and Extension Policies

- What I found most helpful in being successful was knowing I did not have to attend class if I had something else going on and that there were still plenty of ways for me to complete and understand the assignment.
- I think that the most helpful policies were the extension policy and being able to do writing reflections to make up for a missed class… with these policies in place, it encourages students to not give up because it gives them the breathing room they need to catch up.
- I appreciated that we could come to class or choose to do work autonomously.
- I was not able to come to class in person because I didn't have a reliable source of transportation. The course was extremely helpful for me because I could still access all the class material that we worked on during in-person class.
- I loved the due date extension policy.
- I have a terrible time turning things in on time and I am so grateful for the extension policy and flexibility I received.
- I found it very helpful to be able to submit my assignments a few days later if I requested. This allowed me to turn in my best possible work while also not letting me procrastinate. For the weeks that I had a lot going on in other classes or family life, this helped me so so much.

In addition to these responses, I have had many students tell me how the flexible attendance and extension policies helped them learn the material and be successful in my classes, and I have been astounded by the difference this redesign has meant for my students. I would like to end this chapter by sharing Nicki's response to the follow-up question to the survey she took. Here is that question: How has Anti-Oppressive UD design in classroom *structure, policy, practice, curriculum, assignments*, or *assessments* supported your learning or created equitable access to your education in this class?

Nicki's Survey Response to Follow-Up Question

The attendance and extension policies of this class have made it the most accessible I've ever attended. Often I find rigid attendance or extension policies make me much more concerned about my grades than learning the content of the course, but here it was clear the point is to learn in the best way possible. I needed an extension for my capstone essay and it was the first time I have ever asked for an extension without feeling any guilt or like I had to beg, which in turn led me to feel confident in the work I was turning in. As a person, the accommodations and openness made me feel like a person and not a walking GPA generator.

"A Person and Not a Walking GPA Generator"

Empowering students to be a "person and not a walking GPA generator" is exactly what I wanted my Flexible Attendance and Extension policies to do! Again, students cannot learn unless they are free to be fully actualized humans with agency in their creativity and learning.

Chapter 4 Teacher Toolkit Example

It might be helpful to see an example of the Class Materials and the accompanying Writing Reflection assignment that provides an alternative for learning the class material under my Flexible Attendance Policy. This is from my Children's Literature Class.

For the Class Materials, I put links to any videos we watch in class. If I give a lecture or explanation in class, I will provide a link to an alternative reading or video here instead of typing out the lecture or explanation. This makes my creation of the class materials sustainable. In this example, there would be a link to both a video and an article. I'll note that the article is not one that students who attend class are asked to read since they were present for the lecture or discussion. However, I will direct students to the class materials as optional supplementary materials or content they can review. The alternatives in the Class Materials were beneficial to many students, not just ones who missed class. Some students who attended class found it helpful to see the material presented in a different way. A few students would go through the Class Materials even though they attended class because they liked having access to supplementary materials. Some liked being able to easily access the videos to rewatch.

I use the same format for Class Materials as well as the Writing Reflections, copying and pasting the same wording in the frame of the class materials to keep the structure consistent and predictable for students and to reduce my own workload.

For the Writing Reflection, I simply put in any prompts for in-class discussions or writing into the assignment to guide the reflections on the class materials. In this example, the first part is a prompt based on a whole class discussion I facilitate after we watch Kimberlé Crenshaw's video. The second part is a prompt based on an in-class activity where students can choose to participate in a small group discussion or write independently on the prompt.

Here are the examples for one day's Class Materials and Writing Reflections.

View: 2/6 Class Materials
Nothing is submitted here! These are the class materials I went over in class today. If you missed class or would like to review the class materials, please see below.
Today's Class Agenda

1. Watch Kimberlé Crenshaw's "The Urgency of Intersectionality"
2. Class Discussion on Intersectionality

3. Small Group Discussion or Independent Writing on Intersectionality and stories in the *Fresh Ink* anthology.

Content warning: This video contains stories and video footage of violence against Black people by law enforcement.

   ♦ Please watch Kimberlé Crenshaw's Video "The Urgency of Intersectionality"

This video introduces you to the concept of intersectionality by Kimberlé Crenshaw, who was the scholar who first coined the phrase "intersectionality."

   ♦ Optional: Peter Kaufman's "Intersectionality for Beginners"

This optional reading, as the title implies, is a more basic introduction to the concept of intersectionality that might be a helpful supplemental reading.

Submit: Writing Reflections on 2/6 Class Materials
If you attended today's class, then you don't have to do anything! I already gave you credit for this assignment so you do not need to submit the Writing Reflection on Class Materials!
      If you did not attend/do the activities in class, then please follow the directions to complete this assignment.

Preparation for Writing Reflection
First, please make sure that you have done the assigned readings for today's class and have looked through the "VIEW: 2/6 Class Materials" module item in the Week 6 Module.

Prompts for Writing Reflection
This will be a two-part writing reflection. Please label each part "Part 1" and "Part 2."

Directions for Part 1:
Please write a paragraph (roughly 6–8 sentences) on the following prompt: How do Kimberlé Crenshaw's video and Peter Kaufmann's article help you understand the concept of

intersectionality? For example, you can note things that you already knew about intersectionality, comment on new learning about intersectionality, and/or make connections to your own personal experiences or other readings/classes.

Directions for Part 2:
First, choose a story from *Fresh Ink*, edited by Lamar Giles, where you see intersectional identities represented (a character with two or more intersecting marginalized identities).

Next, please write a paragraph (roughly 6–8 sentences) response about why you think it is important to see this intersectional representation in a story.

To submit the assignment, please click the blue "Start Assignment" button on the right-hand side of your screen and then follow the instructions.

Note: This writing reflection will not be commented upon or evaluated. You will get full credit for either participating in class activities or submitting the reflection in Canvas by the due date. The point of the assignment is simply to reflect on what you're learning in class free from evaluation or critique. Therefore, you will *not* be evaluated on the quality of writing, length, or other such considerations. If you are present in class, I will give you credit for the assignment during class time. If you are not present in class and submit your written reflection through Canvas, I will skim your assignment to make sure it follows the prompt, and if it does, I will give you full credit for following the prompt.

If you need an extension, please message me your request before midnight on the original due date.

 Teacher Toolkit Exercise: Class Materials and Writing Reflection for the Flexible Attendance Policy

Ready to try out your own Class Materials and Writing Reflection for the Flexible Attendance policy? Good! Here's your chance. Please feel free to use or adapt my frame for both the Class Materials and Writing Reflection.

Creating the Class Materials

Choose a day's lesson and put that lesson into the Class Materials. Here are some items you might include:

- Daily class agenda
- Reminders or announcements
- Handouts that you passed out in class
- Links or PDFs to articles as an alternative to lectures, explanations, or discussions
- Slide decks or lecture notes
- Links to videos you showed in class
- Links to videos as an alternative to lectures, explanations, or discussions

Creating the Writing Reflections

Create an opportunity for students to reflect on the Class Materials. Here are some prompts you might include:

- Prompt you used in class for discussions or writing
- Prompt you used in class for an activity
- Prompt to reflect on articles or videos or slide decks or lecture notes that are meant as alternatives to in-class lectures
- Prompt to reflect on videos shown in class
- Prompt to reflect on content in a handout
- Prompt to reflect on an upcoming assignment

What This Tool Is For: You can use this tool to design a structure that provides students with equitable access to class materials.

Works Cited

Crenshaw, Kimberlé. "The Urgency of Intersectionality." *YouTube*, uploaded by TED Talk, 7 Dec, 2016. www.youtube.com/watch?v=akOe5-UsQ2o. Accessed 7 June 2023.

Freire, Paulo. *Pedagogy of the Oppressed*, 30th Anniversary Edition. Continuum International, 2003.

Kaufman, Peter. "Intersectionality for Beginners." *Everyday Sociology*, W.W. Norton and Company, 23 Apr. 2018, www.everydaysociologyblog.com/2018/04/intersectionality-for-beginners.html.

Ma, Diana. "Equitable UDL Policies." Dianamaauthor.com, 11 Nov. 2022, https://dianamaauthor.com/equitable-udl-policies. Accessed 18 Nov. 2024.

NCES. Table 1. Public high school 4-year adjusted cohort graduation rate (ACGR), race/ethnicity and selected demographic characteristics for the United States, the 50 states, the District of Columbia, and Puerto Rico: School year 2019–20. IES NCES, National Center for Education Statistics, nces.ed.gov/ccd/tables/ACGR_RE_and_characteristics_2019-20.asp. Accessed 24 July 2023.

5

Reframing Accommodations with Anti-Oppressive Universal Design

Shortly after the COVID-19 school closures in my state ended, I found myself in conversation with a teacher I didn't know well. We chatted briefly about what it was like to return to in-person teaching, and then he asked me, "Aren't you finding that students are more entitled since the pandemic?"

I blinked in confusion. "What do you mean?"

"Students don't even *ask* me for accommodations anymore," he explained. "It's like they just expect me to give them an extension or make my lecture notes available."

Why shouldn't students expect to be accommodated? I was surprised that he would think that students' need for accommodations came out of entitlement rather than a reasonable expectation for support, particularly in the face of inequitable structural barriers like rigid due dates and inaccessible class materials.

Carefully, I replied, "I wouldn't say that students are more *entitled* around accommodations. I think students are more *empowered* in who they are and what they need. That's exciting to me." Exciting is actually a bit of an understatement. I'm *thrilled* that so many students have stopped asking, "Can we have this?" Instead, students are asking, "Why can't we?" This generation is making the world the one they want to live in.

"Actually," I continued, "it gives me so much hope that students are expecting accommodations."

"That's an interesting perspective," the other teacher said politely, but I could tell he had no idea what I meant. Yet, not five minutes ago, he was complaining about the lack of nourishing food options at his school's cafeteria and telling me that "students can't learn if they don't have anything but junk food to sustain them."

I absolutely agreed with him. Students can't learn if their human needs like access to food are not being met. I also believe that students' safety, belonging, and the freedom to be their full selves—are also human needs. So, why couldn't this teacher see that students need accommodations like flexible due dates and access to class materials to learn?

I wonder if the answer lies in how accommodations are framed—not as necessary supports to meet *human* needs, but rather as add-ons requiring extra labor from the teacher to meet *special* needs. I do not believe that students' rights to access, equity, and freedom from injustice are special needs—they are human needs.

This chapter is about reframing classroom accommodations as necessary to meet human needs. I believe that we, as teachers, can work with students to meet both student *and* teacher human needs by using the Anti-Oppressive Universal Design (UD) principles of multiplicity, flexible design, equity, and humanizing pedagogy to build accommodations into the classroom design. These accommodations not only dismantle unjust educational structures but affirm students in their cultures and identities.

This chapter will discuss reframing accommodations to do the following:

- ♦ Dismantle inequity in classroom design
- ♦ Build access and support into the classroom that empower students to freely and fully express their creativity, cultures, identities, and humanity

Why Accommodations Need to Be Reframed

Classroom accommodations are often framed as a matter of legal compliance. By legal compliance, I mean that official accommodations in a student's Individualized Education Plan (IEP) or 504 Plan are mandated by disabilities rights legislation like the Individuals with Disabilities Education Act (IDEA) and the Rehabilitation Act that guarantees disabled students the right to Free Appropriate Public Education (FAPE) under Section 504. IEPs and 504 plans are important legal protections that are necessary for disabled students' right to educational access as are the departments and programs that oversee special education.

However, a system that relies on the legal documents of IEPs and 504s to provide students with accommodations has several issues. Special education and accommodations were created under laws passed through the important work of the disabilities rights movement—laws like IDEA and FAPE under Section 504. These laws created greater educational access for disabled students but did not dismantle the inherently oppressive structure of an educational system built on racism, ableism, colonialism, economic injustice, and sexism. Of course, I am not saying that we should do away with IEPs and 504 Plans. For many students, these are necessary for greater educational access and provide needed legal protections.

What I *am* saying is that we need to recognize the inequities of the current system of accommodations and special education programs before we can build new structures to support students for access, equity, and humanizing freedom. So, let's examine the systemic inequities in the current system.

- Special education that is based on a deficit model results in inequitable educational segregation.
- Special education programs and accommodations focus on the single issue of disabilities rights rather than building an intersectional framework of disabilities justice to dismantle the distinct and intersecting inequities of ableism, racism, economic injustice, sexism, heterosexism, and transphobia.

- Getting accommodations in an IEP or a 504 plan is often a complex and inequitable process that may require shared networking, financial and educational resources, and access to and knowledge of healthcare and legal systems—all of which can be a barrier for students, particularly BIPOC (Black, Indigenous, and People of Color), immigrant, and lower income students and their families.
- IEPs and 504 plans provide *single-user* accommodations with the purpose of creating greater access for an *individual* student rather than *universal* accommodations with the purpose of dismantling structural inequity in classroom design for *all* students.

I recognize that teachers can do little to change larger district procedures that govern IEPs and 504 plans or district-implemented special education programs. Fortunately, we *can* use an Anti-Oppressive UD framework in our classrooms to build new structures that resist systemic inequities.

The Deficit Model of Special Education Is Inequitable

Accessible education is necessary, but the deficit model of special education that segregates students on the basis of abilities is inequitable. This segregated special education is the system that Kyle in Chapter 2 experienced. He spent nearly his entire time at school in a self-contained special education classroom where students with cognitive disabilities were, in Kyle's words, thrown away.

Yet Kyle *was* able to learn in Ms. Lee's Creative Writing class, which was designed not only to accommodate a multiplicity of students but also to resist the inequitable system of special education segregation that impeded Kyle's learning and harmed his sense of self. Ms. Lee taught him with flexible design and with the full belief in his ability to learn because she recognized that it was Kyle's environment that disabled him, not his abilities. Kyle's school deemed him so significantly disabled that he could not learn with his non-disabled or "less significantly disabled" peers—denying him equitable education and the basic human need of belonging.

For BIPOC students, the harm of being confined to self-contained special education classrooms or separate resource rooms is compounded by an oppressive history of educational segregation. One Black student told me that every time he walked down the hall to a special education resource room, he felt overwhelmed with shame. An Indigenous student told me that she learned to feel worthless in the special education she was placed in. An Asian student told me he felt trapped in a self-contained classroom. Anti-black, colonialist, anti-immigrant, and anti-Asian school segregation is baked into the US history of education, and BIPOC students feel the pain of that history in their bones. Confining BIPOC disabled students to a special education system modeled on historical colonialism and educational segregation re-traumatizes students.

Before we can dismantle inequity in special education, we need to recognize the intersectional ways that ableism and racism are intertwined. We need to understand that while there is no such thing as a normal body, there *is* a body that everything is normed on—and that body is white, cishet male, and non-disabled. To design equitable education, schools need a paradigm shift from disabilities rights to the intersectionality of disabilities justice.

The purpose of the disability justice framework is to dismantle not only systems of ableism but also other intertwined oppressive systems such as racism, heterosexism, and transphobia. Activist Patty Berne discusses the disabilities justice framework in their blog post for Sins Invalid, an organization that they co-founded. In that post, Berne acknowledges the importance and necessity of the disabilities rights movement but also points out the limitations. They describe disabilities rights as a "single issue identity based" movement that "has historically centered white experiences" and "centers people who can achieve rights and access through a legal or rights-based framework" (Berne). Disabilities justice, on the other hand, is an intersectional framework that was created by disabled activists of color and that recognizes the "disability experience itself being shaped by race, gender, class, gender expression, historical moment, relationship to colonization and more" (Berne).

In other words, a special education system that focuses only on disabilities rights—and not on undoing the intersecting ableism, racism, sexism, and economic injustice that shapes students' experiences—will never be an equitable system. No student is free from educational injustice unless all students are free. If we are accommodating only students with access to the protections of IEPs and 504s, then we are not addressing the racism, economic injustice, and sexism that underlie the educational system. If we view disabilities rights as the only issue that we are addressing in classroom accommodations, then we are missing the intersections of race, class, and gender that are shaping students' experiences. This intersectional lens is what helped me understand my own experience in school.

My Story

Fifth grade was exciting for me because this was the year that students became eligible for band. I could barely contain my enthusiasm when my parents took me to a band orientation. There, the band teacher let me try out several different instruments before we decided that the clarinet would be the best fit for me. My parents bought me a second-hand clarinet, and I loved the shiny metal keys, the wooden reed, the pages of sheet music, and the velvet-lined case. I couldn't wait to be a part of a band and play beautiful melodies on my new-to-me clarinet.

Then came the day of the first band practice. My classroom teacher announced that all the band students were to report to band practice. All eyes went to a few of us as we got up, picked up our instrument cases, and walked out of the classroom. I felt the heat of the gazes on my back as I left, but I didn't know why I felt so uncomfortable. When we came back from band practice, everyone looked up again, and I experienced the same uneasiness of being watched. I also felt overwhelmed about coming in during the middle of a lesson or activity and being too embarrassed to ask what was going on. The same thing happened a couple more times, and my feeling of discomfort grew worse.

Then for the third or fourth band practice, my teacher made the usual announcement, and the other band students stood up. I knew I was supposed to go with them—but I couldn't move. My forehead beaded with perspiration and heat flooded my face as I tried to get off my chair, but something kept me stuck in place.

It is only now that I am realizing what that heavy *something* was—and also recognizing that it wasn't just one thing. Part of it was my body remembering the feeling of watching other Asian students being forced to leave class to go to their segregated English learner classes. Part of it was the racist bullying by kids who told me I didn't belong and that I was different. But there was more. Recently, I have begun to wonder if I am neurodivergent. It seems likely. When I read about or talk to autistic women about their experiences, particularly BIPOC women, I feel a ping of recognition.

My point is that the message I got in school was that to be different, whether it was in race or neurodivergence or anything else, was a bad thing—and I knew I was different. So, I don't know if it was racism or ableism that kept me in my chair, and that's exactly my point—my experiences could not be separated into neat categories of race and neurodivergence because those parts of me are intersecting and inextricably connected. At the time, I didn't know any of this. All I knew was that I couldn't force myself out of my seat with all those eyes on me.

When the other band kids told me that I was going to get in trouble if I kept skipping band practice, I promised that I'd go to the next practice, fully believing I could and would. But I never did. Instead, I stayed vigilant for signs of my band teacher in the hallways and was ready to go the other direction or even duck behind a library stack on one memorable occasion. I didn't know what was wrong with me—I just knew that it felt physically impossible to leave the classroom with everyone watching me.

Now, I ask myself what it would have taken for me to get out of that chair and go to band class to play the instrument I was so excited about. The answer comes to me quickly. It would have taken a classroom where everyone's identities were respected and affirmed and everyone's different ways of being were valued and supported. In other words, no accommodation in a line or two on an IEP or 504 plan would have gotten me out of that chair. What I needed was a whole new design and framework. I needed to see my diverse identities as an important part of the classroom and not as cause for ostracization and ridicule.

With an intersectional disabilities justice framework, students and teachers can recognize that it is the classroom *design*, not students' own bodies or minds, that creates a barrier to learning. A student who is empowered through a disabilities justice framework sees their disability not as a deficit but as a necessary and valued diversity. As Berne puts it, "A Disability Justice framework understands that all bodies are unique and essential, that all bodies have strengths and needs that must be met. We know that we are powerful not despite the complexities of our bodies, but because of them." A teacher with an intersectional and justice mindset recognizes that they can change the classroom design to remove structural barriers to meet *all* their students' needs because "all bodies have strengths and needs that must be met."

To create a comprehensive equitable design of our classrooms, we need the intersectional framework of disabilities justice that recognizes and affirms multiple intersecting identities of race, gender, gender identity, class, *and* disabilities—not as deficits but as diverse identities. *That* is why I am so hopeful and excited when students come into my classroom empowered in who they are and with the full expectation of being accommodated. More and more students are using an intersectional framework of disabilities justice to advocate for educational change rather than relying on a flawed system to meet their needs. And this change is necessary because the way accommodations are provided and implemented is inequitable.

The Accommodations Process Is Inequitable

Accommodations are necessary, but the process for students to get classroom accommodations and how they are implemented are inequitable. To understand the structural barriers students encounter in getting necessary classroom accommodations, I'd like to share another student response to the same survey that I discussed in the previous chapters.

The response is to the following question: "How did classroom *structure, policy,* teaching *practice, curriculum, assignments,* or *assessments* create a barrier in your learning or access to education in your K-12 experience (especially in middle school or high school)?"

Jan's Survey Response

I went to a school where the curriculum and assignments were very rigid. I was not diagnosed with autism spectrum disorder (ASD) until I was 19 years old and had already dropped out of school. I often had so much homework that I would get so anxious that I would freeze and not be able to complete it. I internalized words like lazy and stupid without even being told once that I was either of those things. Simply by building a culture within the schools where in order to ask for an accommodation you needed a doctor's note or 504 plan (that still had rules for what you are and are not allowed to ask for) to have the accommodation approved. I excelled on almost every test, demonstrating understanding of the materials, so the teachers would often meet my requests with something along the lines of "but you are so smart I don't understand why you can't just do this." I ended up internalizing the ideas that "I just can't do this" and without having an official ASD diagnosis yet it was my understanding that the reason why I couldn't do the tasks assigned was because I was lazy and stupid. Even now, I am so self-conscious of this internalized identity that I soak my assignments in water before tearing them up to recycle them, because I am scared people may look at my thoughts and ideas. To this day I am always incredibly anxious that each quarter might be the quarter that I fail to keep up with my work despite consistently being on the Dean's List and receiving scholarships because that's how much I have internalized these traits that I "can't do school."

I Can't Do School

It was heartbreaking for me to read how Jan ended up dropping out of school. This was not due to Jan's capabilities or her work ethic, and it was certainly not due to innate "deficiencies." Yet, as a result of the inequitable and inflexible design in curriculum that she describes as "very rigid," Jan struggled with school and "internalized words like lazy and stupid without even being told once that [she] was either of those things." In fact, she became convinced that she couldn't do school. What is so painful about Jan's experience is that this was an entirely preventable outcome. All Jan needed was a few flexible changes to be successful in school, but instead the inflexible curricular design led her to believe that she, herself was the one who was deficient—rather than the classroom design.

Jan's gut-wrenching conviction that she could not do school was compounded by her teachers' dismissals when Jan asked for accommodations to keep up with her homework. As Jan put it, an insurmountable barrier resulted "Simply by building a culture within the schools where in order to ask for an accommodation you needed a doctor's note or 504 plan (that still had rules for what you are and are not allowed to ask for) to have the accommodation approved."

Jan's experience is, unfortunately, very common. In fact, the barriers to getting a medical diagnosis and accommodations speak to the systemic inequity in both healthcare and education. Some students and their families lack the socio-economic class privilege to navigate the complexities of those institutions. That might not have been the case with Jan, but her intersectional identities of being a disabled girl did affect her educational experiences. In other words, to understand Jan's experience, we need to acknowledge the complex ways ableism and sexism work together.

In girls and women, ASD is egregiously underdiagnosed (Lockwood et al.) partly because the medical field bases its studies primarily on cisgender boys and men. This is also true of girls with attention-deficit/hyperactivity disorder (ADHD) (Quinn and Madhoo). Jan did not get a diagnosis for ASD until she was an adult and after she had already dropped out of school. She was a girl who did well on tests without any behavioral issues, so her school did not see Jan as fitting the mold of a student who needed accommodations. In other words, ableism and sexism worked together to prevent Jan from receiving necessary accommodations.

All too often, students do not qualify for accommodations because of the inequitable barriers built into the process and then are left with no support in overcoming the inequities and inflexibilities in classroom design. Without a documented disability, Jan faced an inequitable barrier to getting her educational needs met in the classroom.

Unfortunately, classroom accommodations are often seen as something that teachers have the power to "give" and that students are expected to be grateful to receive as if it were some kind of charity. Paulo Freire calls this "False generosity" (44), which "constrains the fearful and subdued, 'the rejects of life,' to extend their trembling hands" (45). The freedom to learn should not be a gift—it should be a goal that both teachers and students are working toward. This structure of teachers "giving" and students passively "receiving" accommodations is dehumanizing and inequitable—in terms of both the authoritarian teacher–student power structure in the classroom and the larger school system.

Schools require evaluations and documentations to measure the extent of a student's disability (and a student's ability to conform to a nondisabled norm) in order to determine a student's need for accommodations. But disabilities have nothing to do with what a student can or cannot do. Disabilities are not about deficits. In other words, disabled students are not *disabled by their disabilities*. Disabled students are *disabled by systems of oppression* that do not allow them to be their full authentic selves and do not value the diversity of bodies and minds. Therefore, any discussion of accommodations must be focused on undoing the harm of ableism rather than making up for any perceived deficits. Accommodations should *not* be used to fix the *student*. Accommodations should be used to fix flawed *educational design*.

This focus on fixing student deficits is another reason that IEPs, in particular, are inequitable in design. While both 504 plans and IEPs contain accommodations, IEPs also provide Specially Designed Instruction (SDI) that has annual student goals that are sometimes measured against non-disabled behaviors and norms and are often provided in self-contained classrooms or mandatory pull-out resource rooms. This is an ableist approach that assumes disabled students need to conform to non-disabled ways of thinking, learning, and being to be included in Gen Ed classes. Disabled students, BIPOC, and Multiple Language Learners (MLL) do not need containment and exclusion to learn—no student does. What students do need is a multiple, flexible, equitable, and humanizing design of curriculum and practice to learn and to be their authentic selves.

It is beyond the scope of this book to get into the intricacies of IEPs and 504s, but I am going to focus my discussion on the accommodations section of both documents. In addition to the inequitable barriers of getting an IEP or 504, there is another major issue with this delivery system for accommodations. The accommodations in IEPs and 504 plans are *single-user* accommodations that might grant an individual student more access, but these accommodations do not create a *universal design* of curriculum and practices to provide equitable access to *all* students.

Equity is not accessible education for *some* students—it is access and freedom in education for *all* students. Therefore, equitable education is where all students' needs (not just "special needs") are met through multiple, flexible, equitable, and humanizing curriculum and practices.

In fact, I do not believe there is such a thing as a "special need." A student who uses a wheelchair and needs to be able to get to their classes does not have a special need. A student who needs food that they are not allergic to does not have a special need. A student who needs insulin shots does not have a special need. A student who needs their textbooks in braille does not have a special need. A student who needs an aide to access the classroom curriculum does not have a special need. A student who needs to be included in a Gen Ed classroom without their teachers and peers questioning their right to be there does not have a special need. The needs for access, food, safety, education, and belonging are not special needs. They are human needs. To call them special is to imply that disabled students are getting an exemption or favor—while ignoring the fact that non-disabled students have the privilege of having their needs recognized as an unquestioned right.

The lack of wheelchair ramps, food for students with food allergies, textbooks in braille, aides, and inclusive classrooms is the result of flawed educational design and inequitable structures that disable students. However, the term "special needs" encourages us to think of the task of accommodating human needs to be something "extra" that schools do rather than what it really is—a necessary part of equitable education.

I also do not believe there is such a thing as *special* education. An education where all students have access to learning and are valued and sustained in who they are is an equitable education. However, special education is a legal term that mandates services, so as a teacher, I'm not focused on changing the terminology that is part of the larger process of education. I'm focused on designing my own classrooms for freedom and equity, and on that note, I want to add one more thing about special education teachers.

Many special education teachers I've met are uniquely trained in flexible and accessible design—yet their knowledge is confined to self-contained special education classrooms and resource rooms. This is another consequence of the deficit model that separates "special education" (where much of the flexible and accessible teaching happens) into the silo of special education. That is unfortunate since the expertise of special education teachers would be valuable in designing equitable Gen Ed classes.

Under the Anti-Oppressive UD framework, we can take accommodations out of the foundation of special education and instead reframe accommodations as necessary equity tools to meet students' human needs rather than "special needs."

Reframing Accommodations as Equity Tools

Currently, IEPs and 504s might be access tools, but they are not equity tools. As Audre Lorde says, "The master's tools will never dismantle the master's house," and IEPs and 504s simply do not dismantle inequitable access to learning in the classroom. Single-user accommodations in IEPs and 504 plans might not create equity, but teachers can reframe them as equity tools by using accommodations to guide Anti-Oppressive UD in their classrooms.

Before my classes even start, I sit down with all the accommodations I've received for my students. Then I make sure that my class is designed to meet the accommodations. For example, my flexible due date policy already accommodates every student with an accommodation for flexible due dates. This means students don't have to be embarrassed to ask me for this accommodation, and this also doesn't require extra work on my part.

If I see an accommodation that I haven't taken into account in my class, then I will redesign my class so the accommodation is part of the class. For example, if I come across an accommodation for a student to have the option of independent work instead of group work, I design this accommodation into the class structure to avoid singling out the one student for a special "exemption." This is a simple redesign. All I have to do is give multiple options for activities requiring group work.

That means students can discuss a topic in small groups or independently write responses to the discussion prompts or read silently if they don't have time to complete the reading being discussed. This redesign to include multiple options for class activities ends up benefitting all students who need multiple options for various reasons. In other words, IEPs and 504s can be used as tools to identify the inequitable structures within the class so teachers can redesign them.

Turning single-user accommodations into universal design is one way to reframe accommodations, but I believe there is more that can be done. As I said, it would have taken an explicit recognition of my humanity and needs to make me feel safe enough to get out of that chair in fifth grade to go to band. And that is why I redesigned my classroom accommodations policy.

Redesigning an Inequitable Accommodations Policy

The accommodations policy I used for many years was copied and pasted from a list of standard syllabus statements that instructors were encouraged to choose from. I simply picked the first one on the list. Here it is:

Disabilities Services

Reasonable accommodations are available for students with documented disabilities. Students should contact Disability Services to discuss their accommodation needs as soon as possible.

What Makes This an Inequitable Accommodations Policy

It is common to discuss accommodations as a matter of legal compliance. In fact, one version of the accommodations policy simply summarized the content of the Americans with Disabilities Act. Even if a policy does not explicitly talk about accommodations as a legal right, most standard accommodations do state the need for students and their families to work with disabilities services to get official accommodations. This can be an arduous process for families, and some are never able to successfully navigate the process to get any accommodations for their students.

What is striking about the version I shared above is the phrase *"documented disability."* Structural barriers sometimes keep students from getting documentation for their disabilities in the first place, which means that they are locked out of the system. Even if families are able to overcome barriers of economic injustice, sexism, and racism to get their students a documented diagnosis of a disability and to then get official school accommodations, these accommodations are then passed onto the teacher as a list of legal requirements. This implies that meeting our students' educational needs is a matter of following a prescriptive checklist. However, creating an equitable and responsive classroom that meets all our students' needs requires more than a checklist.

So, what I wanted to create was a policy that reframed accommodations as necessary to meet *human* needs and create equitable design—rather than a checklist of legal requirements. Here is my redesigned accommodations policy.

My Statement on Accommodations

My belief is that we ALL need accommodations. What we need to be successful in our learning will be different from person to person, and

I believe that acknowledging and valuing those differences will make our class more powerful and rewarding. Therefore, I am committed to making individualized accommodations under an Anti-Oppressive UD framework for equitable access to education. I recognize that there are structural barriers preventing students from accessing their education, and I do not view accommodations as an exception, a handout, a special exemption, or a favor. Instead, I view accommodations as necessary tools to dismantle the inequities in our educational system. I have put many of these Anti-Oppressive UD policies and practices into the design of the course, but I believe in working with you, so please let me know what accommodations you need to access the class fully. I am always learning in collaboration with students to design equitable and sustainable accommodations.

What Makes This an Equitable Accommodations Policy

One thing that makes this policy equitable is that I am not requiring that students go through a complicated and inequitable process to get an IEP or 504 in order for me to provide accommodations. I am making clear that it is structural barriers, *not* students' deficiencies, that make accommodations necessary. I am drawing from the principle of *humanizing pedagogy* when I say that "acknowledging and valuing" different ways of learning and being "will make our class more powerful and rewarding." I am also designing this policy under the principles of *equity* when I say that "I do not view accommodations as an exception, a handout, a special exemption, or a favor" and that "I view accommodations as necessary tools to dismantle the inequities in our educational system." It is inequitable and dehumanizing to make students justify or prove their need for access and for me to center my power and authority to provide that access. Instead, my redesigned policy creates an environment where we are working together to dismantle structural barriers through *multiple* and *flexible* accommodations.

The accommodations I make in the classroom are ones designed in collaboration with individual students. For example, I had a student who had a part-time job and had a hard time with weekday due dates. She didn't want to request an extension for each assignment and felt an overall Saturday due date would work better for her, but she was reluctant to ask for an individualized due date because she saw it as a "special exemption."

There was an easy and equitable solution, and it started with letting go of an equality model and the idea that every student had to have the exact same structure. Embracing the principles of multiplicity, flexible design, equity, and humanizing pedagogy, I told my student that the design of the class was *flexible*, so I would be happy to change all her individual due dates to Saturday at midnight without requiring her to request an extension. As I assured my student, there was absolutely no reason that students had to have the same due date. *Multiple* options were necessary so students can get the structure that works for them. This was a structure that was sustainable for me as well because one or two students who turned in all their work on Saturday didn't negatively affect my grading load.

Not only was I able to be responsive to the needs of individual students with Anti-Oppressive UD, but I was able to make this a sustainable practice. All it took was normalizing accommodations as *human* needs we *all* have—including my own needs.

In fact, the next chapter will talk about reframing accommodations to build sustainable teaching. For now, however, I would like to end this chapter with Jan's story and her response to the follow-up question to the survey she took. Here is that question: "How has Anti-Oppressive UD design in classroom *structure, policy, practice, curriculum, assignments,* or *assessments* supported your learning or created equitable access to your education in this class?"

Jan's Follow-Up Survey Response

For me, the course policy was so helpful. When I get anxious, with my ASD I have a full body shut down. To ask for an extension on work or accommodation sometimes takes me hours if not several days to build up the confidence to ask for one. Simply by creating an expectation that everyone has different needs and it is okay to engage in self-advocacy to get those needs met, reduced my anxiety so much that even when there was a very high level of work to juggle, I was able to turn my assignments on in time and make it to every class. I have really made a lot of progress in un-internalizing a lot of the negative traits I have adopted because of my ability to keep up with the coursework assigned. A big reason for this, I feel like, is because I have seen that the culture of the class impacts my work so much more than my abilities and I have been able to see that I am actually able to juggle a lot of work without even needing to go through hoops for accommodations. I still feel that anxiety when I start a new class, but in the back of my mind I can remind myself that I have done well in college courses before so I can do it again.

I Can Do It Again

I can't express how moved I am by Jan's response. Jan was a student who, as a result of an inequitable and rigid educational structure, truly believed that she "can't do school." However, it did not take much for her to start unlearning that script. All it took was a multiple, flexible, equitable, and humanizing classroom design that, as she said, created "an expectation that everyone has different needs and it is okay to engage in self-advocacy to get those needs met." I love Jan's statement that "the culture of the class impacts my work so much more than my abilities" because it shows that she realizes there is nothing in her that needs to be fixed. All the obstacles she has encountered and that caused her to drop out of school were due to flaws in educational structure. *That* is what needed to be fixed. Jan now believes she *can* do school without losing her wonderful spirit, creativity, and humanity.

In short, accommodations can be normalized simply by reframing them as necessary to meet human needs—for students and teachers.

Chapter 5 Teacher Toolkit Example

As I said, single-user accommodations on IEPs and 504s can be reframed to identify inequitable barriers within the classroom curriculum and practices. In this chapter, I gave an example of how I took a single-user accommodation of having the option to work independently instead of with a group and used this accommodation to create Universal Design by adding multiple options to class activities.

In fact, many of my equitable policies and practices come out of single-user accommodations that I've used to identify ways to create Universal Design in the classroom. Here is a table of examples of how I've turned single-user accommodations into Universal Design.

Single-User Accommodation	Universal Design
Option to work independently during group work	Multiple options for class activities
Extra time for assignments	Equitable Extension Policy
Excused medical absences	Flexible Attendance Policy
Access to slides, lecture notes, and other class materials	Class materials posted in online course management system

Teacher Toolkit Exercise: Using Accommodations to Redesign Inequitable Curriculum and Practices

Now it's your turn to use single-user accommodations to identify areas that can be redesigned with Anti-Oppressive UD!

Prompt: How can you use your students' single user accommodations to design equitable and accessible curriculum and practices to meet all your students' multiple needs?

♦ **Directions**: First, use the single-user accommodations in your students' IEPs and 504s to identify opportunities for Anti-Oppressive UD. Then redesign curriculum and practices to be multiple, flexible, equitable, and humanizing. Once you finish, your teacher toolkit will contain a redesigned curriculum and practices that accommodate both the students with the IEP or 504 and also other students who need education designed with the principles of multiplicity, flexible design, equity, and humanizing pedagogy. In other words, you will end up with a curriculum and practices designed to accommodate *all* students.

What This Tool Is for: You can use this tool to reframe accommodations as equity tools.

Works Cited

Berne, Patty. "Disability Justice - a working draft by Patty Berne." *Sins Invalid: An Unashamed Claim to Beauty in the Face of Invisibility*, Sins Invalid, 10 June 2015, www.sinsinvalid.org/blog/disability-justice-a-working-draft-by-patty-berne. Accessed 19 Oct. 2024.

Freire, Paulo. *Pedagogy of the Oppressed*, 30th Anniversary Edition. Continuum International, 2003.

Lockwood Estrin, G., Milner, V., Spain, D. et al. Barriers to Autism Spectrum Disorder Diagnosis for Young Women and Girls: A Systematic Review. *Rev J Autism Dev Disord* 8, 454–470 (2021). https://doi.org/10.1007/s40489-020-00225-8. Accessed 5 August 2024.

Lorde, Audre. "The Master's Tools Will Never Dismantle the Master's House." *Sister Outsider*. Crossing Press, 2007.

Ma, Diana. "Reframing Accommodations." Dianamaauthor.com, 11 Nov. 2022, https://dianamaauthor.com/reframing-accommodations/. Accessed 18 Nov. 2024.

Quinn, Patricia O., and Manisha Madhoo. "A Review of Attention-Deficit/Hyperactivity Disorder in Women and Girls: Uncovering This Hidden Diagnosis." *The Primary Care Companion for CNS Disorders*, vol. 16, no. 3, 13 Oct. 2014. National Library of Medicine, www.ncbi.nlm.nih.gov/pmc/articles/PMC4195638/. Accessed 3 July 2023.

6
Building Sustainable Teaching with Anti-Oppressive Universal Design

Whenever I attend professional development talks and workshops, the topic of sustainable teaching hardly ever comes up—and when it does, the discussion usually turns to measures like mindful meditation or suggestions for self-care. Now, I'm all for mindful meditation and self-care, but none of these outside measures is enough. Sustainable teaching shouldn't be an add-on that teachers do to cope with the stresses of the classroom—it should be baked into the classroom design.

An anti-oppressive framework is actually a sustainable teaching model because it challenges the authoritarian "banking" education that confines teachers and students into fixed and unsustainable roles. According to Paulo Freire, a traditional "banking" education is one where the teacher is the active "subject" who deposits knowledge into the student, the "object" who passively receives this knowledge. This banking education is oppressive because it dehumanizes students *and* teachers, reducing students to compliant receptacles and teachers to mechanical dispensers. This is certainly *not* how I want to interact with my students.

What I *want* is to build relationships with my students to engage them in their learning and uplift us all. As Freire puts it,

> True generosity lies in striving so that these hands—whether of individuals or entire peoples—need to be extended less and less in supplication, so that more and more, they become human hands which work, and, working, transform the world. (45)

Fortunately, that is exactly what Anti-Oppressive Universal Design (UD) allows me to do. By building multiple, flexible, equitable, and humanizing education, teachers and students can break free of our fixed roles and work together to sustain each other's humanity.

This recognition of my own humanity is what I needed when it came to grading. For much of my teaching career, I felt like a grade dispenser. My job was to enforce the school expectations and dispense grades quickly and efficiently—all without expressing human need. That was why I always handed back graded work within a week and took a day off only in cases of extreme illness. I got in the habit of lugging around a folder of ungraded papers wherever I went so I could grade while I waited for a friend at a lunch date or in my doctor's office. I even graded when I was on bed rest for my first pregnancy. If I was behind, I would stay up late at night or cancel plans to meet my self-imposed deadline.

What I did not do, was ask for an extension. It did not matter if I was sick or tired or simply wanted to spend time with a friend. In my mind, the deadline was a fixed entity and had to be met at all costs. Never mind that the cost was my physical and mental health or relationships with my children, family, and friends.

Of course, grading wasn't the only deadline I had. As teachers, we tend to have a lot of deadlines, whether it's grading, school paperwork, or emails to answer. If we happen to be teachers *and* parents, then the responsibilities multiply. Many of us have other responsibilities as well, but I never felt I could bring my individual struggles or needs into the classroom. I felt that to do so would be to admit that I was a bad teacher—because I had a life outside the classroom and was, therefore, not a perfect machine.

But here's the thing. Machines might be needless, but humans are not. We have needs, wants, hopes, histories, cultures, interests, joys, passions, and dreams—and none of those things makes us deficient or means that we need to be fixed. One of the most dehumanizing functions of the traditional education machine is that it requires students and teachers to deny our own needs to keep the machine running.

Anti-Oppressive UD allows teachers to bring our full, authentic selves to our teaching. Teachers are not machines, so we must create a structure that acknowledges our humanity and supports teaching practices that work for us as much as they work for our students.

Teachers Have Human Needs

I have found that being transparent about my own needs in the classroom makes it more likely for my students to communicate with me about their own needs. For example, now I occasionally let students know that I need an accommodation of a little more time to grade their assignments. And when I do, I remind them that they should feel free to let me know if they need more time on assignments—normalizing accommodations.

I believe it is important to communicate my own needs because if I don't, I might unintentionally create inequitable policies and practices in an attempt to meet those needs. For example, my former strict and rigid classroom policies on attendance, late work, and accommodations were inequitable because they were designed to reinforce my authority in the classroom, but if I examine them more deeply, I can see there are unmet needs that these policies were hiding.

Looking at my former class policies, I see a long list of "Thou shalt nots." Almost every policy started with a "No" or a "Don't." For example (and I'm paraphrasing here to keep this concise, but this list captures the spirit of my old class policies):

- ♦ No food or drink in class.
- ♦ No cell phones in class.
- ♦ Don't turn in work past the due date.
- ♦ Don't plagiarize.

However, when I examined my class policies through the lens of the Anti-Oppressive UD principles, I realized that all those "no" and "don't" statements were hiding what *I* needed. I needed a classroom free of crumpled wrappers, spilled soda, and a fine dust of crumbs over everything, which I then felt I had to clean up. I needed to be free of the distraction of students texting on their phones in the middle of my lessons in order to teach effectively. I needed a way to manage the large amount of late work that came in so I wouldn't feel overwhelmed. I needed a way to deal with the inordinate drain on my time and energy when it came to plagiarism.

There is certainly nothing wrong with having those needs. Again, to have needs is to be human. The problem was that I wasn't *acknowledging* those needs. Instead, I was covering up being overwhelmed and anxious with policies that framed student behaviors as disrespectful, irresponsible, or dishonest. My students' *behaviors* weren't the issue—my unmet needs were the issue. Again, we all need accommodations, and that includes teachers. Instead of trying to fix my students' behaviors through strict classroom policies, I had to find a humanizing way to get my own needs met.

The first two (food/drink and cell phones) were not relevant in the pandemic-era virtual classes, but I actually found these two issues to be fairly simple to address even when I got back into the classroom. I was up-front with my students about the fact that I get overwhelmed when I'm confronted with a mound of garbage I need to hurriedly clean up before the next class. Then I asked if everyone could help clean up the class before they left. Instead of lecturing students about responsibility and disrespect, I was transparent about my needs and asked if we could make cleaning up a community responsibility. I was surprised to find how well this worked.

When I had made cleaning up an individual responsibility, there was always one or two students who would forget to throw away their trash, but once it was a group effort with everyone participating, it all got cleaned up. I wasn't focused on teaching about responsibility, so I didn't care who picked up what. That wasn't the point—I had an unmet need disguised as a classroom rule, and once that need was met, there was no longer a reason for a strict no food/no drink policy. That policy is no longer on my syllabus.

Cell phones, the second issue, is one that's getting a lot of attention lately with schools implementing schoolwide bans on cell phones. I do understand how cell phones can be a distraction and have certainly struggled with this in the past. However, I was personally so relieved to get back into a physical classroom with students that I found I wasn't as bothered as I used to be when those students were on their phones.

Still, I do talk about phones with my students. I say that I understand there are many reasons students might need to have access to their phones, but also that I worry that I'm boring students if I see them on the phone. I realized that the issue with cell phones is not my concern that they are a sign of disrespect. My concern is that cell phones are a sign of disengagement, and it's *this* worry that distracts me from my teaching.

Once I understood that, I realized that my unmet need was actually one of communication. I tell students all the places my mind goes to when I see students on their phones. *Are you bored with this lesson? Confused? Do you have a sick cat and are waiting for results from the vet?* It's no wonder I get distracted!

Now, I ask my students to let me know if they need to have their phones out so I'm not distracted by wondering if it's something about my teaching that isn't engaging them. Students come into class and let me know if they're waiting on a text or call about something important. Some say they find it helpful to take notes on their phones. Some say that they use their phone to look up things if someone makes a reference they're not familiar with. At this point, no one has told me that my class just isn't a priority and they'd rather scroll through cat memes rather than engage in the class.

This communication is what I need to do my job as a teacher successfully, and it's amazing how this accommodation has alleviated my anxiety and level of distraction. That is why I no longer have a cell phone policy on my syllabus. However, I want to be clear about something. Just as the accommodations each student needs to learn are individualized and multiple, so are the accommodations each teacher needs to teach. In other words, this specific accommodation might not be what *you* need to address the issue of cell phones.

I believe the key to creating accommodations that work is to figure out what unmet needs we have in the classroom, be transparent with students about our own needs and theirs, and work collaboratively to meet everyone's needs through multiplicity, flexibility, equity, and humanizing pedagogy. I have a feeling that the teacher who complained about students acting "entitled" to accommodations in the previous chapter had his own unmet needs.

This brings me to the third item on my former "Thou Shalt Not" list—the Late Work policy. I have learned that students are less likely to want to do something if it starts with a "Don't." In fact, I suspect many of us tend to bristle at being commanded and restrained. That's why policies phrased as "Don't turn in work late" are not very effective, and they are definitely not humanizing. However, if a policy or rule starts with a "Can" rather than a "Don't," then I'm much more willing to do it. Naturally, our redesigned policies cannot simply rephrase an inequitable rule to make it more likely that students will comply with it. However, the policy can be redesigned to recognize the humanity of both teacher and student and be rephrased as a request for an accommodation. And the first step is to remove the "Don't."

I already talked about how I redesigned my Late Work policy into an extension policy in Chapter Four, but now I want to discuss how I made this into a sustainable policy.

Making Policies Sustainable

I realized that my previous inflexible policy of "no late work" resulted from my unmet need for structure and of being able to anticipate my grading load. Once I understood this, I was ready to revise my policy to make it sustainable for me. When I talk to my students about the extension policy, I tell them that I have created a process that makes it clear and straightforward. I know many students get anxious when the process is unclear or there is not enough structure. (I do too.)

However, I *also* know structure is not the same as rigidity. Just as my students and I need transparent structure, we also need flexibility. I've tried to include that flexibility in my extension policy. I have also made it clear that I designed the process to be sustainable for me and *not* to teach students "responsibility" or to prepare them for the "real world." Here are the parts of my extension policy that I have specifically redesigned as a process that is sustainable and acknowledges my own humanity as a teacher.

- *Please make extension requests before midnight of the assignment due date. It can be difficult for me to manage my grading load effectively if I receive unexpected extension requests after the assignment has closed. It also helps me anticipate my grading load when I can anticipate when assignments are going to come in. Of course, I understand that mistakes or life circumstances happen, so please do let me know if something kept you from making the extension request on time. Again, extension requests made before midnight of the due date will be automatically met and do not require an explanation/reason for the request.*
- *Please understand that the default extension is 48 hours (although I'm happy to discuss a longer extension if you need it). My concern with longer extensions is that it could put you too far behind to get caught up or create a domino effect that keeps you perpetually behind. In this case, I will work with you to balance giving you extra time to complete assignments without jeopardizing your success with future assignments.*

In addition, I put the following reminder in each assignment: "If you need an extension, please make sure to message me your request before midnight on the original due date." None of this is an attempt to establish my authority in the classroom. I am simply being up front with students that I am also human and need a sustainable process for *all* of us.

This process has worked well for my students and me because it has multiple and flexible options and is equitable and humanizing. This is not a rigid model that seeks to fix students' "deficiencies" in study skills or work completion. Other teachers have different processes that work for them and their students. My point is that there is no one way to accommodate all students or teachers just as there is no one way to meet all human needs. What matters is that we have an equitable, humanizing way to communicate our needs.

This brings me to the last policy on my former list of "Thou Shalt Not" class policies—and that is my plagiarism policy.

My former plagiarism policy was probably the most punitive and strict policy I had, and this was a direct reflection of how large my unmet and unacknowledged need was. There are few things as exhausting as searching for the source of a plagiarized assignment, documenting it, and then reporting it. This could easily take hours of agonizing and heartbreaking work, and I hated doing it, but I saw no other way to address plagiarism than reinforcing this inequitable policy.

Like my previous accommodations policy, I believe my plagiarism policy, at least partly, came from a template that either my school or my department provided. Here is that policy:

Standard Plagiarism Policy

Plagiarism is the intentional use of someone else's words or ideas without giving that person credit. This includes submitting someone else's essay in its entirety or in parts as your own, using any words, phrasing, and/or ideas from a source (this includes the internet) without proper citation, having someone else write your paper or assisting so much that the phrasing and ideas are no longer your own, and re-submitting an essay previously written for another class. Plagiarism is absolutely prohibited and will result in receiving a "0" on the paper and possibly discipline on the part of the college administration. Failure (intentional or not) to give credit to your sources will result in failure of the paper. We will discuss this in class and work on examples in order to clear up confusion and concerns.

Why This Is an Inequitable Policy

This plagiarism policy is inequitable because it focuses on changing student behavior without ever addressing the structural barriers that keep students from being successful. In my experience, students generally do not plagiarize because of laziness or innate dishonesty. Students plagiarize because they don't understand the assignment, don't feel they have the skills to meet the assessment criteria, don't have time to do the assignment, or are experiencing some other barrier. Therefore, the issue can be addressed by designing assignments, assessments, teaching practices, and extension policies to be flexible, multiple, equitable, and humanizing.

Punitive policies might change student behavior but they will do nothing to fix the systemic root of the problem. Another reason that a punitive plagiarism policy is inequitable is that it is often BIPOC (Black, Indigenous, and People of Color) students and Multiple Language Learners (MLL) who are accused of plagiarism. Fortunately, despite the disparity between my written work and my silence in the classroom, I was never accused of plagiarism. I suspect that was partly due to the model minority myth that casts Asians as rule-abiding, passive, model students. However, I know Black colleagues and students who had also never plagiarized and were equally good writers—and yet they *were* accused of plagiarism.

The disproportionate number of Black students who receive punitive discipline speaks to racism and anti-Blackness in our policies. White students plagiarize too, but they are less likely to get "caught" because their proficiency with White Mainstream English is assumed. That is a privilege that BIPOC and MLL students (especially those with the intersectional identity of being BIPOC immigrants) do not have. Any policy that perpetuates the racism of its disproportionate impact is an inherently an inequitable one.

I have to admit that it took a painful experience for me to realize just how damaging and inequitable my plagiarism policy was. Some years ago, I was making my way through an unending pile of composition essays when I came across a plagiarized essay by a student who happened to be Chinese.

At the time, my policy stated that I would give a "0" on any plagiarized essay and report the student for school discipline. I felt that I had no choice but to follow the standard department plagiarism policy.

Unfortunately, I didn't even consider that my student might be encountering structural barriers of racism or economic injustice. That might have had something to do with a workshop presentation I had recently attended on understanding and serving international students. This seemed like a useful topic, but I was surprised to find a problematic underlying message about Chinese international students in particular. The implication was that we, as teachers, should hold Chinese students to rigorous standards because they were mostly rich teens who were in the US to party rather than to learn. Needless to say, I was uncomfortable with these assumptions, but I didn't speak up because I didn't want to seem overly sensitive as one of the few Chinese American teachers at the workshop.

Yet it didn't occur to me that I had internalized the racist messages of this workshop when I gave my student a "0" on his essay. After all, in failing my student, I was treating every student *equally* although not *equitably*. An equitable policy would have taken structural barriers of economic injustice and racism into consideration—and my policy definitely did not.

Several days later, I got an email from my Chinese international student that felt like a gut punch. My student apologized profusely and told me that his parents struggled to work multiple jobs in China so they could send their only child to an American school in the hopes of a better future. He wrote that he was ashamed to think of what they would say if they knew what he had done.

I was mortified to realize I *had* internalized those racist messages from the workshop by assuming my student was privileged and not serious about his education. My student was not some spoiled, rich kid caricature who didn't care about his education. He was a very human student who didn't have time to read the book and didn't understand the assignment. He had plagiarized out of desperation, not entitlement, which is probably true of most students.

In other words, it was not the innate flaws in my student that led him to plagiarize—it was the flawed design of my class. At the time, I did not have an equitable extension policy, flexible options in assignments, a multiplicity of texts, or policies that recognized the humanity of my students.

My punitive plagiarism policy kept me from recognizing and affirming not only my students' humanity but my *own* humanity as well. This became clear as I agonized over how to address my student's plagiarism. My heart was telling me to give him a chance to rewrite his essay, but I was torn. What about my plagiarism policy? Wouldn't it be unfair to the other students if I made an exception to the rules? These, of course, were the wrong questions and false choices. The *real* question was how I could design structures that would eliminate such false choices and support both teachers and students.

Not surprisingly, I did end up giving my student an opportunity to rewrite his essay. However, I could have saved my student and myself quite a bit of heartache if I had only designed a humane and sustainable process in the first place. The truth was that we both needed an alternative to the unjust and inhumane system that we were trapped in. My student felt like his only choices were to plagiarize or fail to complete an assignment. And I felt like my only choices were to make a special exception or penalize my student with a failing grade. Fortunately, there *is* a way to move beyond these false choices. Anti-Oppressive UD could have helped me redesign my plagiarism policy to resist dehumanization and instead affirm my students' and my *own* humanity.

However, I could not redesign my plagiarism policy until I acknowledged my unmet need. I don't think I'm overstating it to say that dealing with plagiarism (especially now with generative artificial intelligence [AI] programs like ChatGPT) makes me feel like I am fighting a time-, energy-, and soul-sucking beast. Partly, this is due to the fact that I am both a writing teacher and a writer—my own writing and my voice are important to me, and I want my students' writing and voices to be important to them too.

The problem was that my original policy didn't acknowledge my own need for accommodations and instead framed plagiarism as expectations of ethics and honesty that would be punished if breached. I could not design an equitable and humanizing policy until I acknowledged my own humanity. My need for a sustainable way to conserve my time, energy, and spirit had to be addressed in any redesign. In my new statement, I have revised the plagiarism policy and reframed it into an accommodation I need.

Reframing Classroom Policies as Teacher Accommodations

Realizing that my punitive classroom policies like my former plagiarism policy were the result of my own unmet needs helped me understand how I could redesign them. I realized that I could normalize the language of accommodations by acknowledging my own needs and also reframe authoritarian class policies as teacher accommodation, so that's exactly what I did. Here is the explanation I put on my syllabus about my list of teacher accommodations. I have also included an example of one of my teacher accommodations, which is actually my redesigned plagiarism policy. My full list of teacher accommodations is in the Teacher Toolkit Example at the end of this chapter.

Accommodations I Need

We all need accommodations, so in an attempt to normalize the language of accommodations, I will be transparent about what I need to be successful as your teacher.

- ♦ *Take ownership of and honor your own voice, ideas, and writing. Your voice, ideas, and writing are important. Plagiarism (the intentional use of someone else's words or ideas without giving that person credit, including submitting someone else's writing as your own, using any words, phrasing, and/or ideas from a source without proper citation, having someone else write your assignments or assisting so much that the phrasing or ideas are no longer your own, and using a generative AI program to write your assignments) takes up an inordinate amount of my time and energy. Our school has a discipline policy that includes getting a "0" on the assignment and disciplinary action from the office of Student Services. I absolutely dread going through that process—not only because it's a lot of work on my part, but because it's painful to take disciplinary action against a student. This is a disciplinary process that I do not intend to participate in again. Please work with me to avoid a situation that's not good for any of us. Keep in mind the class extension policy—I encourage you to use it if you need more time on an assignment for any reason. If you find yourself overwhelmed or unsure about an assignment or class design, please reach out so we can figure out how to make the assignment or class design doable and avoid having you resort to using someone else's ideas or words.*

Why This Is an Equitable Policy

This example shows how I have revised my former list of "Thou Shalt Not" class policies into a list of teacher accommodations. In fact, the redesign of my plagiarism policy that starts with "Take ownership of and honor your own voice, ideas, and writing" is just one accommodation in a longer list of teacher accommodations. Again, in the Teacher's Toolkit Example at the end of this chapter, I'll provide the full list of my teacher accommodations as a model you might borrow from.

When I first drafted this revision, I thought about leaving out the part about the larger school plagiarism policy, but in the end, I decided it would be disingenuous to ignore the existence of a punitive school-wide plagiarism policy. Again, there might not be much that teachers can do about the inequitable policies that govern schools; however, we *can* refuse to be an unquestioning cog in the machine of traditional education, and our classroom policies can state that. This is an equitable policy because it does not frame plagiarism as a matter of student's personal responsibility or ethics, nor does it focus on "fixing" these assumed deficiencies with authoritarian restrictions.

My former plagiarism policy was a "Don't" policy—*Don't plagiarize*. What my policy did not say was what students *could* do. My policy had no options for expression or empowerment in writing. For a writing teacher and a writer, that seemed to be a huge oversight. That is why my redesigned policy removes the "Don't" and starts with what students *can* do: "Take ownership of and honor your own voice, ideas, and writing."

There has been a lot of talk about generative AI lately, and that topic would take a whole other book to fully address. I will just say here that if AI chatbots had been around when I used my former plagiarism policy, then it certainly would have been included in the policy. I am equally certain that a policy that relies on punishment as a deterrent would have been wholly inadequate in preventing the use of AI to write assignments. Again, the focus of an Anti-Oppressive UD framework is not to change student behaviors but to empower them in their own learning and to be free in the expression of their true humanity—which includes being free from the machinery of AI.

However, we cannot empower student expression and freedom through restrictions. What we *can* do is empower students through designing curriculum and practice under the Anti-Oppressive UD principles of multiplicity, flexible design, equity, and human pedagogy.

Normalizing Accommodations

Many students have told me that my transparency about my own need for accommodations encourages them to be open about their own needs. In fact, I asked students that exact question on a survey. Here are the questions I asked about accommodations:

1. Would you agree that the "Statement on Accommodations" (providing everyone individualized accommodations as part of my commitment to equity) on the syllabus made it more likely that you would communicate with me about your need for accommodations in the class?
2. Would you agree that the "Accommodations Your Instructor Needs" statement in the syllabus normalized the language of accommodations and helped you ask for the accommodations you need in this class?

3. Would you agree that the framing of the class policies as the "Accommodations Your Instructor Needs" statement in the syllabus made the class policies welcoming and understandable?

About 90% of students agreed with these three statements, roughly 10% were "not sure," and no one disagreed with any of these statements. What is interesting is that the third question about framing the class policies as "Accommodations Your Instructor Needs" had the highest percentage of students agreeing with that statement—roughly 95%. This was heartening to me because it showed me that I could transform punitive policies into "welcoming" ones simply by reframing those policies as accommodations I needed. As I said in the previous chapter, it is exciting that students are empowered to expect accommodations in a system that needs fixing. It is also encouraging to me that my transparency about my needs in the classroom also supports my students' freedom to express themselves.

For example, I recently taught a lesson on privilege and oppression that I needed to modify to accommodate my needs. This was an activity where students identify for themselves what privileged identities and what oppressed identities they had. I've always found it helpful to model this process by identifying my positionality in these socially constructed categories like socio-economic class or race (middle class in the category of socio-economic class and person of color in the category of race).

Normally, I go through all nine of these socially constructed categories and explain my process in identifying whether I have privilege or experience oppression (privilege in the category of socio-economic class and oppression in the category of race). I explain that this process has been useful to understand my identities in terms of both privilege and oppression.

This time, however, I told students that I was still on my journey to understand my identity in two of these categories, so this framework of privilege and oppression did not reflect the nuance and complexity of my exploration. Because of this, I explained that I would not be modeling my process of analyzing these two identities with the binary framework of privilege and oppression.

Instantly, a student raised her hand and said, "I just want to say that it is so inspiring to see you be open about this. It makes this classroom feel safe for *me* to be who I am."

There were murmurs of agreement, and then students started sharing about their own discoveries about who they were and the ways they have struggled to be understood in those identities. Over and over again, the theme that came up was how free and supported they felt to express themselves in my class. That was such a beautiful moment, and it was made possible by this space we built together. I fully trusted and believed in my students and in our ability to care for each other. My class was an Anti-Oppressive UD community designed with the principles of multiplicity, flexible design, equity, and humanizing pedagogy. There was enough space here for my students and me to be human and have our needs met.

Chapter 6 Teacher Toolkit Example

In this chapter, I talked about the necessity of teacher accommodations, so I'd like to share the accommodations I need in the classroom. Of course the accommodations you need to be your fully authentic self in the classroom will most likely be different, but here is my list of accommodations.

Accommodations I Need

As I said, we all need accommodations, so in an attempt to normalize the language of accommodations, I will be transparent about what I need to be successful as your teacher:

- *Understand that I need holidays and weekends off, so I will stop checking or responding to student messages at 3 p.m. on Fridays. I will resume responding to student messages on Monday morning.*
- *Allow me a full 24 hours on instructional days to respond to your messages. If you don't hear from me after 24 hours on instructional days (not on weekends or holidays), please message me again.*

- *Use Canvas messaging (the "Inbox" icon on the left hand navigation bar in Canvas) to contact me. Although individual assignments allow you to leave "submission comments," I don't see those submission comments unless I'm actually grading your assignment. Therefore, if you want to be sure that I get your message, please send me a standard Canvas message, using the "Inbox" icon on the left-hand navigation bar in Canvas.*
- *Understand that you might receive a form response (indicated in the syllabus) to common questions and issues. I set up the form responses to help me respond quickly to the many messages I receive. It is not meant to be impersonal; it is simply an accommodation I need to manage messages. I do read all student correspondence and try to respond within 24 hours on instructional days.*
- *Allow me a full week to grade your assignments. If you don't see your assignment graded after a full week, please let me know. If I need longer than a week to complete my grading, I will let you know through a class announcement.*
- *Let me know before midnight of the original due date if you need an extension. Understand that I have set up the process to make it possible for me to accommodate the many extension requests I receive, so please try to follow this process to keep it sustainable for me.*
- *Take ownership of and honor your own voice, ideas, and writing. Your voice, ideas, and writing are important. Plagiarism (the intentional use of someone else's words or ideas without giving that person credit, including submitting someone else's writing as your own, using any words, phrasing, and/or ideas from a source without proper citation, having someone else write your assignments or assisting so much that the phrasing or ideas are no longer your own, and using a generative AI program to write your assignments) takes up an inordinate amount of my time and energy. Our school has a discipline policy that includes getting a "0" on the assignment and disciplinary action from the office of Student Services. I absolutely dread going through that process—not only because it's a lot of work on my part, but because it's painful to take disciplinary*

action against a student. This is a disciplinary process that I do not intend to participate in again. Please work with me to avoid a situation that's not good for any of us. Keep in mind the class extension policy—I encourage you to use it if you need more time on an assignment for any reason. If you find yourself overwhelmed or unsure about an assignment or class design, please reach out so we can figure out how to make the assignment or class design doable and avoid having you resort to using someone else's ideas or words.

♦ *Communicate with me to let me know what you need to be successful. Since I can't anticipate all the educational barriers that each individual student faces, it's helpful for me to know what's keeping the class from being accessible and equitable for you in order to figure out useful accommodations.*

♦ *Understand that I will be making and taking accommodations under a collaborative model. Accommodations need to be sustainable for all of us, so they might not be exactly how you envisioned, but please be open to collaboration as we work together to make the class an equitable and transformative experience for all of us!*

 Teacher Toolkit Exercise: Creating Your Own Teacher Accommodations

Now it is time to create your own teacher accommodations. Here are the steps we're going to take to create that list to get your needs met and be free to be your fully authentic, humanized self in the classroom.

1. The first step in creating teacher accommodations is to make a list of your own unmet needs in the classroom. As I said in this chapter, many of my original rigid and punitive class policies came about because of my unmet needs. In case you need some examples, I'll recap the unmet needs I shared in this chapter.

- My need for a clean classroom free of messes I had to clean up at the end of each class period
- My need to be free of the distraction to my teaching that cell phones caused
- My need to manage and not be overwhelmed by a large influx of work submitted after the deadline
- My need to conserve time, energy, and spirit in the face of a draining process to deal with plagiarism

2. The next step is to decide which of your unmet needs could be addressed with a redesign of classroom practice. That was what I did with my original "No Food and Drink" and "No Cell Phone" policies. This redesign of classroom practice, however, took a dialogue with my students to come up with a collaborative solution that worked for all of us. Your dialogue with your students may very well likely result in a different redesign of classroom practice, which is fine as long as it is designed collaboratively with the Anti-Oppressive UD principles of multiplicity, flexible design, equity, and humanizing pedagogy.
3. Now, you are going to decide which of your unmet needs can be addressed with a redesign of classroom structure. This is what I did by redesigning my late work policy into an extension policy.
4. At this point, you will probably still have some unmet needs on your list that can be addressed by reframing an existing classroom policy as a teacher accommodation instead. A few, like my plagiarism policy, will take a careful rethinking of what it is that you are asking students to do. I had to reflect on this for a while before I could figure out how to redesign my "Don't plagiarize" policy into an accommodation request to "Take ownership of and honor your own voice, ideas, and writing." You might want to put these thornier ones aside to think about and start with the policies that are easier to reframe.
5. The last step is to create teacher accommodations from the remaining unmet needs. You might want to go to your existing class policies and see if you can revise them

into teacher accommodations. Many of my class policies were actually fairly easy to redesign into teacher accommodations. As I mentioned, most of my classroom policies started with a "Don't," so all I needed to do was start with a "Do" that made my own need for accommodation transparent. For example, the first accommodation on my list used to be a class policy that said something like this: "Please don't message me on weekends or holidays. I will not respond to messages received over weekends and holidays." There isn't anything particularly punitive or harsh about this statement, but simply the framing of it as a rule rather than an accommodation I am requesting creates an inequitable power structure. With a slightly revised wording in the form of an accommodation, my statement now reads, "Understand that I need holidays and weekends off, so I will stop checking or responding to student messages at 3 p.m. on Fridays. I will resume responding to student messages on Monday morning." With this revision, I am acknowledging my own need for time off and asking for understanding. In fact, more than one of my accommodations start with "Understand" because what I am asking for is an understanding of our mutual humanity.

What This Tool Is For: You can use this tool to redesign inequitable policies *and* get your teacher and human needs met in the classroom.

Works Cited

Freire, Paulo. *Pedagogy of the Oppressed*, 30th Anniversary Edition. Continuum International, 2003.

Ma, Diana. "Reframing Accommodations." Dianamaauthor.com, 11 Nov. 2022, https://dianamaauthor.com/reframing-accommodations/. Accessed 18 Nov. 2024.

7

Building Equitable Assignments and Assessments with Anti-Oppressive Universal Design

I have always loved teaching, but grading? Not so much. Maybe it had something to do with how I used to take a bag filled with student papers or a laptop wherever I went in case I got a spare moment to grade. I grew used to the ghosts of ungraded assignments constantly hovering over my shoulder, but sometimes it felt like most of my life was consumed by grading (or the guilt of not grading).

When I heard my students talk about their *own* stress about the assignments hanging over their heads, I realized that no one was finding much enjoyment in this ongoing cycle of assignments and assessments. I couldn't help but think there was a better way to approach this process.

Of course, now I *do* believe there is a better way. I think the first step is to recognize that traditional education is a machine that treats students' creative work and thinking as objects to be assessed rather than expressions of their identities, cultures, and learning. Fortunately, we can use the Anti-Oppressive Universal

Design (UD) principles of multiplicity, flexible design, equity, and humanizing pedagogy to create assignments and assessments that create freedom of expression and engagement for students *and* teachers.

In this chapter, I will talk about using Anti-Oppressive UD in the following ways:

- Centering the multiplicity of student voices and choices
- Making assignments and assessments flexible and sustainable
- Engaging students in the assignment and assessment process

The Anti-Oppressive UD framework allows teachers the freedom to design assignments and assessments according to the principles of multiplicity, flexible design, equity, and humanizing relationships between teachers and students. The Anti-Oppressive UD framework is *not* a "one-size fits all" template or a prescriptive set of directives. Instead, the Anti-Oppressive UD framework is meant to guide and support your *own* design of assignments and assessments that empowers you and your students. After all, there are certainly enough restrictive educational templates and directives out there.

Prescription and Standardization Are Not Equitable Design

It seems that every year there's a new trendy initiative proposed in the name of equity—whether it's a common rubric or labor-based grading. We, as teachers, are expected to get on board with these initiatives and invest hours in training and implementation. And yet, these prescriptive practices all have the same inevitable result. Some students benefit from the new practice—and some don't. Needless to say, this is not equity.

Recently, in a workshop on Anti-Oppressive UD, I asked participants to do a brief activity. First, I presented a slide of different assignment and assessment practices:

- Labor-based grading
- Portfolio or project-based grading
- Using transparent grading rubrics
- Removing grading rubrics
- Grade "norming" for consistency
- "Ungrading" (detailed feedback instead of points and grades)
- Assignment norming
- Assessment with writing/essays rather than quizzes/tests
- Assessment with quizzes/tests rather than writing/essays
- Reducing the number of smaller assignments to reduce busy work and focus on outcomes
- Increasing the number of smaller assignments to focus on process rather than product
- Weighting larger assignments to be worth less to prioritize labor and effort
- Weighting larger assignments to be worth more to reduce workload

After presenting this slide, I asked participants what they would think if they were told to choose *one* "best practice" to adopt as the central equity practice for the entire school. As soon as I asked this question, the workshop participants burst into laughter; it was ludicrous to think that there could be *one* most equitable practice. Although we were laughing, many of us actually have been asked to serve on similar committees or task forces where our job was to identify one practice as the best practice for equity. In fact, some of these "best" practices directly contradict each other. How are we supposed to pick one over the other or decide which ones we should get rid of?

Yet I've been in many workshops or meetings where someone has declared, "Quizzes are inequitable" or "Rubrics are inequitable," and suddenly, we're arguing about whether we should do away with quizzes and rubrics despite the reality that some students would rather demonstrate their learning with a quiz than an essay or that some students need a grading rubric to understand the assessment criteria.

The point is that educational design has often been about *subtraction* when it really needs to be about *multiplication*. Students need multiplicity, flexible design, equity, and humanizing pedagogy in assignments and assessments to counter the structural barriers they face in racist, ableist, and classist systems. Picking one form of assessment over another is not the answer, because it is larger systems of inequity that creates structural barriers, and it is those systems we must be aware of in our assignment design.

I believe that when we talk about inequitable assessments, we often default to arguing that the form of the assessment is inherently inequitable—leading to statements like "Quizzes are inequitable!" However, I find that questioning the *form* of the assessment is not sufficient if we are not also interrogating racist, colonialist, and ableist mindsets behind the assessment.

The truth is that no one form of assessment is completely equitable.

However, practices like labor-based grading have been touted as an equitable assessment that schools are encouraged to adopt. It certainly *seems* more equitable to grade the labor a student does rather than a handful of high-stakes assignments or tests that are subjectively graded.

But what about the student who is working an after-school job to help pay their family's bills? Or the student who understands the concepts but takes twice as long as some of their peers to complete work? Or students who experience other structural barriers to do the required labor? These students need a way to demonstrate their learning and understanding of the concepts that is not solely dependent on the amount of work they produce. For some students, it might actually be more equitable to be assessed on the quality (as subjective as this is) rather than the quantity of their assignments.

Of course, the answer is *not* to switch to an assessment that is based on only a midterm and final test. My point is that there is no *one* equitable assessment. That is why assignments and assessments need to be designed to be multiple and flexible as well as being equity-minded and centered on humanizing pedagogy.

Later, I will provide concrete examples of how to design equitable assignments and assessments rather than simply changing the form of the assessment. But first, I'd like to share a personal story to show why it is necessary to examine the larger structures of racism, economic injustice, and ableism that lead to inequitable assessments.

Understanding the Roots of Inequitable Assessments

In our sophomore year of college, my friend Cass and I took an Art History class. Both of us are Asian—Cass is Vietnamese, and I'm Chinese. We both spoke fluent English and were good students. I had never received below an A on an essay (including the upper-level literature classes I was taking), and Cass had never received below a B on one.

Then, one day, we were assigned a fairly basic Art History essay. Neither of us was concerned about it. Cass wasn't worried because I was in the habit of helping her edit her essays, and I wasn't worried because if I was confident about anything, it was my writing.

Our essays were graded by a teaching assistant (TA) and returned to us, both marked with multiple corrections in red ink and without a single comment on content or organization. I got a B and Cass got a C– grade. We were confused, especially since many of the "corrections" didn't actually correct an error. In most cases, the TA simply substituted a word for one of her own or added a superfluous comma. At the time, it didn't occur to us that our grades might be due to racism. We assumed that we must have missed a crucial element of the assignment, so we went to talk to the TA about our essays. To our surprise, she told us that we had fulfilled every requirement, confirming that our grades were solely due to the "errors" in our writing.

Even then, we *still* didn't get what was happening—not until she said sympathetically, "It takes time to learn English. As Asian students, you shouldn't feel bad that you need help to improve your writing."

We got it then.

Cass and I talked later about how unfair and awful our TA was, but we mostly tried to forget it had ever happened. We both felt a deep sense of shame in being mistaken for Multiple Language Learners (MLL). Even though I was born in the US and Cass had immigrated to the US when she was four, we were both raised with our native languages (Chinese Mandarin for me and Vietnamese for Cass), so we started school in the US with more familiarity with our native languages than with English. Neither one of us was technically an MLL student, but that didn't stop us from internalizing the shame of our languaging that was so inextricably connected with our racial identities.

What we didn't recognize at the time was the inequity of how MLL students were being assessed. Although we understood our TA's racism, we did not fully understand the overall structure of racism that trapped us all. The internalized shame from this incident was profound and lasted beyond this one assignment or even this one class—even though the outward consequences seemed minimal.

Despite that B on a paper, I got an A in the Art History class because the bulk of our grade was based on memorizing a bunch of facts and regurgitating them on a final exam. Neither the paper nor the exam taught me anything about art history that I could recall beyond my final exam, which is yet another problem. However, assignments and assessments that were irrelevant to my learning were so common that it didn't even register in this case.

Cass doesn't remember the grade she got in this class, so it was clear that the class grade made no lasting impression on her. Still, I had the feeling that the assessment of her writing had left a mark. After drafting the story of the Art History TA for this book, I texted her to ask, "Would it be fair to say that the experience affected your confidence in your writing?"

Cass replied immediately: "Definitely!!!" She went on to say, "I met the assignment rubric, and her changing my sentences for her own liking when the sentences were fine was ridiculous."

We exchanged a few more texts about the incident, and then Cass texted, "I know I'm not a great writer."

This pulled me up short. My heart ached to know that after all this time, my friend still felt the consequences of a dehumanizing assessment that saw her only for perceived flaws in her writing. Cass *is* a great writer. Not only is she clear and sharp in her writing, but she is also funny, spirited, bright, and warm—and all that and more comes through in her writing.

But our Art History TA took away Cass's confidence in one assessment.

For years, the most salient aspect of that incident was the TA's individual racism. It took me longer to understand the more insidious problem. This TA thought that she was treating us fairly by holding us to "high standards" and that those random red marks she made on our papers were *helping* us. For the moment, let's ignore the multiple studies that show students simply don't learn how to write through copious amounts of grammar corrections or that there weren't any substantive errors for her to correct in the first place or that she wasn't a trained composition teacher. The TA truly believed she was doing the right thing. And she believed this not because she was a bad person or innately prejudiced but because this is exactly what she was taught to believe.

My misguided Art History TA was likely trained to ferret out and correct deficiencies in students. In other words, she was trained under the traditional education deficit model that sustains the belief that those with marginalized identities are lacking or less than or, at best, are to be pitied. The TA's assumption about our "flawed" writing was due to her own racism. However, the expectation that all student writing should be graded against standards of what April Baker-Bell calls White Mainstream English (WME) was a problem of the traditional education system that perpetuates racism, ableism, and colonialist thinking.

As long as assignments and assessments are designed to "fix" students, these assignments and assessments will be inherently inequitable. Culturally responsive training to help teachers like my Art History TA to recognize implicit bias certainly would have been useful—but it would not have changed the structural inequity of assessing student writing against standards of WME. In other words, there is no equity or recognition of the multiplicity and humanity of our students' voices if we are forcing those voices into constraints normed on white, cishet, non-disabled standards.

The point of the story is not this TA's individual racism, as bad as it was. My point is the problem in *design*. Our learning was being assessed with a "one size fits all" assignment and assessment that were not based on concrete learning outcomes of the class. If there had been clear outcomes for the assignment (like demonstrating an understanding of the difference between Rococo and Baroque art), then perhaps our TA would have assessed our work on those outcomes rather than defaulting to a deficit model assessment.

More importantly, if the assignment had been designed with multiplicity, flexibility, equity, and humanizing pedagogy to be meaningful for students' learning, expression, and creativity, then it would have been an assignment designed for freedom. However, before we can design assignments for freedom, we need to understand what structural barriers we need to break down to create equitable access for students. To that end, I want to share two brief student responses to the following survey question: "How did classroom *structure*, *policy*, teaching *practices*, *curriculum*, *assignments*, or *assessments* create a barrier in your learning or access to education in your K-12 experience (especially in middle school or high school)?"

Student Response 1

Many classes had heavy reading and busy work style assignments that I never even tried to complete. I often cheated because I could memorize answers from others work way better than I could sit and read 45 pages of a textbook. Also a lot of teachers just assigned reading and passed out work packets instead of engaging with students and helping kids who didn't absorb information from non-fiction readings.

Student Response 2

We would have lots of assignments to do for each class. I won't say it's not worth it, but it will let us not be able to have time to learn what we like.

Designing Assignments for Equity and Freedom

These two responses were particularly helpful for me to reflect on because I used to assign a lot of readings in the name of rigor and many small assignments to hold students accountable for the readings. Rigor and accountability are not necessarily negative, but the problem arises when structural barriers keep students from completing "heavy reading" and "busy work." It is inequitable to expect students whose families struggle to pay the electricity bill or students who don't absorb information easily through reading or students dealing with the daily effects of structural racism to be confined to the same inflexible curriculum as students who have the socio-economic, nondisabled, white privilege to conform to rigid standards of rigor and accountability.

I want to point out that when I critique rigid standards, I'm not arguing against necessary standards of *learning*. I am talking about an inequitable curriculum design that mistakes heavy reading and busy work for high expectations and meaningful learning. There are many ways to learn, and some students *do* learn through long readings and smaller assignments that scaffold their understanding of concepts. These kinds of assignments should remain an *option* for students, but there should be other options like learning from handouts that condense information or from peers.

I find it interesting that the student in the first response characterized their memorization of facts from their classmates' work instead of reading from a textbook as "cheating." I imagine some of their teachers would agree, but if we look at this situation through the lens of multiplicity and flexibility, we can see that this student *is* actually learning the concepts of the classes. They're just learning in a different way than the single method of reading many pages from a textbook.

Smaller assignments like notetaking, vocabulary lists, and outlining can also be helpful to scaffold students' learning, but again, the curriculum should be flexibly designed to make these assignments *optional*. The term "busy work" comes up a lot when I talk to students about barriers to their learning. It's not surprising that students don't value work designed to keep them busy. Students, like *all* of us, value work that is meaningful. Yet, students who resist busy work are often characterized as "lazy" or "noncompliant." Neither is true. The second student response points out that this resistance to busy work actually reflects students' *engagement* in learning. They state that lots of assignments keep students from having "time to learn what we like." Students are not resistant to work in general—they are resistant to work that is not meaningful or that does not reflect their interests.

Students are not cogs in the traditional education machine, so assignments should not be dehumanizing work designed to keep them busy. Students are thinking and feeling human beings with their own identities and interests, so assignments should be designed to be student-centered and to empower students to express their full humanity.

Centering Student Voices and Choices in Assignment Design

While there are many ways to design more equitable assignments, one of my favorites is to design a capstone project assignment as the final assessment of each themed unit. Capstone projects allow for multiple and flexible ways for students to demonstrate understanding of the unit concepts. It is also equitable to assign fewer but more meaningful assignments rather than requiring students to do many small and less meaningful assignments that they might not need or have the resources, time, or capacity to complete. Capstone projects can also be designed to be humanizing by centering students' choice and voice so students can work on a project that reflects not only their learning but their cultures, identities, and interests.

Of course, teachers can still build the scaffold of smaller assignments as optional and ungraded work—that is part of the flexible design that is so important to the Anti-Oppressive UD framework. Students learn differently, and teachers can create flexible pathways for students to gain the skills they need to complete a capstone project.

Another thing that I like about capstone projects is that they can be clearly and transparently structured to connect to themed units and to learning outcomes—both the state standards and the student-centered and humanizing learning outcomes teachers might have created for their classes. For example, here are the learning outcomes that I introduced in Chapter 3, "Building Equitable Curriculum and Practices with Anti-Oppressive UD":

- Understand the multiplicity and importance of diverse, intersectional representation.
- Demonstrate responsiveness to a multiplicity of cultures, identities, and histories.
- Express and sustain the student's own cultures, identities, and interests in ways that are meaningful to the student.

I'll provide an example of a capstone project assignment based on the above outcomes in the Teacher Toolkit at the end of this chapter, but here I'd like to discuss why it's important to have these alternate learning outcomes. An outcome like "Demonstrate responsiveness to a multiplicity of cultures, identities, and histories" might not be found on a state standard, but it can provide crucial guidance in designing assignments. This is an outcome I keep in mind when I design assignments that ask students to reflect on the importance of diverse representation.

Here is what one student says in response to a survey question about how the design of my class supported student learning: "The assignments really opened my eyes about a lot of things. I never really noticed that growing up there were never really any books for African American people." I appreciate that this student not only identified that it was valuable to learn about a multiplicity of cultures and identities, but also noted that the assignment design supported that learning.

With the structure of learning outcomes, teachers can also create multiple options for a capstone project that allows for student-centered choice. However, I recognize that there is no way to include all the options that would engage each individual student, so I always have an option for students to propose their own idea to meet the learning outcomes of the assignment.

Most students choose one of the options I assigned, but a few do propose their own project. Here's what one student said about this option in a student survey about the Anti-Oppressive UD of the class and the flexible design elements that contributed to their success in the class.

Student Survey Response

For my capstone project, instead of writing a lesson plan or children's book, I was approved for an alternative project. Since I work with families and children, I created a resource guide to support families in building a diverse book collection. The guide included many of our class resources as well as books and authors we talked about in class. I felt more accomplished and successful that I was creating something that was applicable to both my academic and professional life. I can also use it as a guide for the people I work with to help them look at their libraries with fresh eyes. It was a lot of work, and while I am still polishing it, it was worth it!

It Was Worth It

I love how the student designed her own incredible and meaningful project! I can also say that I enjoyed reading and grading it. Not incidentally, capstone projects are also more sustainable for teachers to grade. Before I taught my first high school class, I used to wonder why teachers didn't assign long essays anymore. The answer became painfully clear the first time I collected my first batch of 150 essays. At that time, it took me roughly 20 minutes to grade and give feedback on each essay.

I'll share how I've made grading sustainable later in the chapter, but at the time, it took me about 50 hours to grade a batch of essays if I collected them all at once from all my classes. If I wanted to get students their essays graded within a week, that meant I needed to grade for approximately seven hours a day on top of the time I spent teaching in the classroom, preparing lesson plans… and grading all the busy work I assigned to make students "accountable." It's no wonder teachers don't assign long essays. We don't have time to grade them.

However, if teachers drop the requirement of busy work and instead design student-centered assignments in the form of capstone projects, then students have time and engagement to create work that is meaningful to them and their learning. Teachers will also have the time to give meaningful feedback if they are not consumed with grading a constant deluge of small assignments.

Redesigning an Inequitable Grading Rubric

It is not just assignments that can be designed with Anti-Oppressive UD principles of multiplicity, flexible design, equity, and humanizing pedagogy. We also need to redesign assessments with Anti-Oppressive UD. Again, getting rid of any particular form of assessment is the wrong focus. Instead, we need to address the underlying foundation of inequity in our assessments.

Take grading rubrics. Yes, it's true that rubrics often contain inequitable criteria, but getting rid of rubrics will not address the inequitable criteria being used for grading. In fact, my Art History TA never gave us a grading rubric, so her assessment of our conformity to what April Baker-Bell called WME was based on a secret criterion that she wielded without the guardrails a transparent rubric would have provided.

So, the question should not be whether or not grading rubrics are inherently inequitable. Rather, we should be asking what oppressive systems are shaping the *design* of our grading rubrics. Again, I feel there isn't any method of assessment that is inherently equitable. That is why we need to design our assessments with intentionality, using the principles of multiplicity, flexible design, equity, and humanizing pedagogy.

One simple thing I did in my grading rubric redesign was to provide students with the choice to opt-out of the rubric. All students needed to do was drop a note in the submission comments to let me know that they did not want me to fill out a rubric. For these students, my plan was to give them a holistic grade that was not broken down into criteria. I do not believe I have had a student opt out of a grading rubric yet, but I still think it's important to give students that option. While the opt-out choice was a simple addition, I knew that redesigning my rubric criteria would be more difficult.

A number of years ago, I took a hard look at my rubric criteria to evaluate how *I* was grading to perpetuate norms of WME. Obviously, my grading rubrics didn't actually contain the phrase "White Mainstream English," but that is the insidious nature of WME—it asserts its dominance by its very invisibility. WME is naturally assumed to be the norm, so it does not need to be named. However, naming WME gives us the ability to see it for what it actually is—a racist, colonialist, nationalist structure that limits students and devalues BIPOC (Black, Indigenous, and People of Color) voices.

It was only by naming WME that I could see the inequitable nature of my grading rubric—especially in the last criterion on my rubric, which was "Writing Conventions: Grammar and spelling should be standard and correct." Of course, I now know that words like "conventions," "standard," and "correct" are often used to disguise WME. It was the criterion that was worth the least amount of points, and I had always included it with a sense of shame in my gut.

However, I felt I had no choice but to grade on "standard" language. As a new teacher, I knew my assignments and assessments were being scrutinized and evaluated. I knew I had to include a criterion about grammar and spelling, and my wording was no different from what other teachers in my department used. In fact, some in my department gave "correctness" of language much more weight and graded much more harshly in this area. Still, I always hated grading on grammar, and it never felt right. It wasn't as if taking points off for misplaced modifiers, comma splices, or sentence fragments was helping anyone approximate WME any better. All it did was convince students that their own languaging was inferior to a standard they would never be able to reach. That was what happened to my friend Cass.

Essentially, the reason that grading on "standard" use of language didn't feel right is that it *wasn't* right, just, or equitable.

Once I realized this, I knew I could not continue to inflict that same damage onto my own students. However, redesigning my rubric was not as simple as taking out that criteria about grammar and spelling for the simple reason that I work under larger school structures.

Most teachers work for schools that require us to assign grades based on course standards, so we sometimes need to contend with larger state standards that are inequitable. To give one example, here is a Washington State Learning Standard in the area of Language: "Demonstrate command of the conventions of standard English grammar and usage when writing or speaking" (Common Core State Standards [CCSS] for English Language Arts [ELA] 51). I have learned to view words like "conventions" as code for WME, so I knew that it was inequitable and dehumanizing to force students into a restrictive standard that insisted on conformity to white-centric conventions. We can't ignore those standards, but we *can* still honor a multiplicity of voices and use flexible design to create an equitable and humanizing assessment tool.

In the "Teaching Tool Exercise" section at the end of this chapter, I'll provide guiding questions for you to design an equitable grading rubric. For now, I'll share how I redesigned my grading rubric with the principles of multiplicity, flexible design, equity, and humanizing pedagogy.

First, I removed the original criterion of "Writing Conventions" from my grading rubric. I did not want to treat my students as passive receptacles who were expected to simply accept the grading criteria. I wanted them to be free to express their full humanity, unrestricted by inequitable criteria... even though we had course standards to meet. To create more flexibility in my criteria, I replaced "Writing Conventions" with the more open criterion of "Clarity of Writing" and the following wording for that criterion: "Writing is clear and understandable." Basically, I assess the "Clarity of Writing" criterion to honor a multiplicity of voices, and by "honor a multiplicity of voices," I mean I tell students upfront that they will get full points in this category as long as their writing is clear enough for me to get a sense of their meaning (and it always is).

I also revised my "Style and Tone" criterion, which used to read something like: "Writing should be in academic style and tone." Now, the description is worded with more openness to read something like: "Writing demonstrates thoughtful choices in the use of style and tone for the writing task." I also give full points in this category because I want to center the student's choices in their writing rather than evaluate them based on a fixed and white-centric standard of "academic" style and tone.

Since designing for freedom is an ongoing process, I know I can be even more explicit about the humanizing pedagogy part of the Anti-Oppressive UD framework. To that end, I am planning to add a "Voice and Vision" category (with guaranteed full points) to affirm students' own voice, vision, agency, and *humanity*. My goal is to create a rubric where students get full credit in a few non-evaluative categories so they get at least 50 percent of the points simply for submitting the assignment.

I want to be clear that I am not "lowering standards" in using Anti-Oppressive UD. Rather, I am using *flexible design* to resist standards rooted in the dominant norms of WME and centering *equitable* standards that recognize a *multiplicity* of voices. The removal of the "correct and standard English" criterion is done under a *humanizing pedagogy* that frees students from the restrictive expectations of traditional education and honors our students' cultures, identities, languages, and experiences.

Not incidentally, it is amazing how clearly, thoughtfully, and beautifully students learn to write when they have agency, engagement, and freedom from dominant norms that restrict them. In fact, once I became more flexible in my assignments and assessments, I found that my students' writing skills grew in proportion to their agency and confidence. Naturally, the process of rubric design will be different in other disciplines and also from teacher to teacher. My overall point is that grading rubrics are not immutable. We create them, so we can also change them.

Assessments, however, are not just points and grades. Assessment can take the form of written feedback. Of course, I did not want my feedback to be the kind of red-ink corrections that my Art History TA made on my essay. I wanted my feedback to be thoughtful, helpful, and encouraging. This, as you might imagine, was not easy.

For many years, I was trying to teach through copious and substantive feedback—and that took time and energy. To compound this issue, some of my students weren't even *reading* my feedback, and those who were reading my feedback expected a justification for their grades. For example, students would ask for an explanation if my feedback didn't address why they lost a point in one of the criteria.

I wanted to meet my students' needs, so I tried to use my feedback to anticipate these questions about their grade. Soon, my feedback no longer became the teaching tool I envisioned and became more of a grade-justification tool. It got to be exhausting, and I wasn't sure if my feedback was helping my students. How could I give useful and individualized feedback if I didn't know what they wanted to know about their own writing? Did *they* even know?

To make matters worse, I had the sinking feeling that the feedback I was giving my students was focused on "fixing" the deficiencies of their writing because no matter how many positive things I said about their writing, I was basing my feedback on how they fell short of the grading criteria. This was not only inequitable but dehumanizing—not the kind of feedback I wanted to give.

In short, my students and I were mired in an inequitable and unsustainable assessment—they were writing toward the grade, and I was giving feedback to justify the grade. This had to change, but I knew the solution was not to remove the necessary transparency that the grading rubric provided. Instead, I had to design a new method of giving feedback that was multiple, flexible, equitable, and humanizing for all of us.

Redesigning an Inequitable and Unsustainable Feedback Process

I realized that the key to redesigning my feedback process was to create multiple options for feedback and to engage students in the feedback process. I used to urge students to read my feedback carefully because it haunted me that I had spent so much time and energy writing feedback that students only skimmed if they read it at all. Then I realized something very basic—I need to stop trying to change student behaviors to fit my expectations. Some students simply do not want individualized written feedback, and I need to understand that their uninterest in my feedback is not necessarily a lack of engagement with their learning. Then again, I could also redesign my feedback process to engage students more fully.

These realizations resulted in two major changes. First, I stopped randomly giving individualized feedback. Instead, I filled out a rubric for every student (unless they opted out of the rubric) and gave a grade based on the rubric criteria. Second, I involved students in the process so I was no longer guessing at what feedback they would find useful. Instead, I asked students to give me questions I could use to guide my feedback. This shifted the focus of my comments from justifying their grade to addressing the questions they had about their own writing—creating agency and engagement.

The big bonus here is that this made my grading both more sustainable and enjoyable. I was giving individualized written feedback to only those who wanted it (roughly 60%–80% of students), and the feedback I gave felt responsive rather than evaluative because I was directly addressing the questions students were asking about their writing rather than arbitrarily deciding what feedback students would find valuable for their writing.

Here is the wording I use in my assignments:

Directions for Teacher Feedback

In the "Submission Comments" box, please write a brief process letter reflecting on the process of writing the essay.

If you're having trouble coming up with something to write in the process letter, here are some prompts you might use to guide your reflection (don't feel that you need to address all of them or any of them, actually): What did you learn through writing the essay? What class activities were helpful in writing the essay? What do you feel you did well in the essay? What was challenging about writing the essay? If you were to continue working on the essay, what would you want to work on improving?

At the end of the process letter, please write two or three questions for me to use as a guide for instructor feedback. This will ensure that my comments will be focused on what you have identified as useful for your own writing and learning.

If you're having trouble coming up with feedback questions, here are some examples of questions you might ask (feel free to use or adapt these or come up with different questions): Did my thesis make an arguable claim and how could that claim be stronger or clearer? What did you think worked particularly well in my essay? Did my examples seem to support my points well, and where could I have used more examples? How did my organization work, and how could I make my essay flow better or make my ideas easier to follow? Did you learn anything or gain a new perspective from reading my essay, and what was it that you took away from my essay?

Also in the process letter, please let me know if you want to opt out of the grading rubric. If you don't specifically opt out, I will go ahead and complete a grading rubric for you. If you do opt out of the grading rubric, I'll simply give you a numerical grade without the breakdown of points in the rubric.

If you do not submit a process letter with instructor questions for me, I will assume that you do not need/want feedback from me at this time, and I will give you the following form comment. (But don't worry if you decide that you want feedback after all! As you can see in the form comment, you can still ask for feedback at any time.)

> *Thank you for submitting your essay. Please refer to the grading rubric for the breakdown of points. Please also message me through Canvas messaging if you have questions or would like feedback. Keep in mind that I don't check the comments in the "submission comment" box after I have graded the submission, so the best way to contact me is through Canvas messaging.*

This student-centered assessment has not only made my grading enjoyable and sustainable but also resulted in students feeling empowered about their own writing. Here, for example, is a student response from a student survey about how Anti-Oppressive

UD supported their success: "I appreciated the process letter for feedback on essays. It felt nice to get feedback that was relevant to what I wanted to know more about rather than what you wanted to tell me." I love the agency and engagement in this response!

I recognize, however, that written feedback is not always possible or even relevant to every discipline. As a writing teacher, I admit that I used to feel a bit smug about not giving tests because I felt that they were an inherently inequitable form of assessments. I was convinced that they assessed test-taking skills rather than understanding or knowledge, and I was determined to not use tests or quizzes in my classes.

I changed my mind when I saw how many students preferred taking quizzes to demonstrate their understanding rather than writing more time-intensive essays. I realized I was not designing under the principle of multiplicity if I simply refused to give quizzes. I talked to teachers who showed me that quizzes could go beyond generic multiple-choice questions from a testing bank and could be designed to assess the specific content and concepts being taught.

I was encouraged by what I was learning about testing assessments, so when I began teaching classes outside the discipline of English, I decided to assign quizzes and shorter writing assignments to give students the opportunity to demonstrate their understanding of the concepts in a less labor-intensive way than writing formal essays. At first, I ran into all the issues that led me to denounce quizzes as inequitable in the first place. My quizzes, as carefully designed to reflect the content of my course as they were, still measured test-taking skills.

Eventually, I came to the same realization with quizzes as I did with grading rubrics. Yes, quizzes are inequitable, but I could redesign my quizzes with the Anti-Oppressive UD principles of multiplicity, flexible design, equity, and humanizing principles. Before I could redesign my quizzes, however, I had to identify the barriers that students experienced in test-taking. To do that, I turned to student surveys that asked students about structural barriers they encountered in assessments. Many of the responses are about quizzes, and here are a few of them.

Student Response 1

Most tests were about regurgitating information, so I would memorize answers and make stuff up to fill in missing information, rather than demonstrating real comprehension. Also I always tried to finish my tests as soon as possible because I have poor time management skills and I would be so stressed about not finishing in time, which often happened, that I would hurriedly fill out things to at least get something on the paper. I would be the kid that would need extra days at the computer filling out questions and doing reading. But I found that embarrassing so I would just guess and try to keep up with other kids.

Student Response 2

I hated anything timed. I didn't realize I had social anxiety until way later, and I am getting help with it now. But I was always stressed and that impacted my learning and I did way worse on tests than on the homework.

Student Response 3

Another thing that negatively affected me was timed tests. I grew anxious at the time and tended to forget everything I studied for and blanked, though once the test was over, all the information would come back, and I would become more stressed.

Redesigning Inequitable Quizzes

The common barrier in all of these responses was the stress of timed tests. In fact, extra time on tests is a common accommodation on Individualized Education Plans (IEPs) and 504s. However, as the student in the first response indicates, the single-user accommodation for extra time on tests causes embarrassment because the student is singled out. The solution has to be a classroom or assessment design to accommodate not just a single student—but all students. Yes, teachers can simply decide not to give tests, but what about the student who needs the structure of a dedicated block of time in the classroom to complete an assessment? I've talked to quite a few students who have trouble completing assignments on their own and tell me that they need the stress of a timed test to motivate them.

These opposing needs might seem like an impossible dilemma, but it can be solved with multiplicity and flexible design. There isn't any one right solution, but an option would be to have a timed test and then allow students to either submit their test at the end of class or take it home to complete. By offering the option to everyone, it builds in the extra-time accommodation into the design of the assessment rather than singling out students with IEPs or 504s for the accommodation.

In fact, this strategy could also be used for students who have a hard time completing essays. Teachers can build in a day where students bring in their texts, notes, and handouts to write an essay. Those who need a test structure for motivation can complete the essay during this workday and submit it. Others can treat it as a non-stressful workday and submit their essay at some later due date.

Another strategy might be to offer the option of an untimed online test option or a writing response. There are many possibilities when designing with multiplicity and flexibility, but I'll share one more. This is an option I add to untimed quizzes, and here is the wording I use to explain the Flexible Quiz Review process to students.

Flexible Quiz Review

I recognize that quizzes are not necessarily the most equitable of assessments as they tend to measure test-taking skills rather than content knowledge, so I have put a quiz review policy in place. If you miss a quiz question due to a misunderstanding of the question or concept, please feel free to submit a quiz review.

In the quiz review, you will be asked to follow these three steps for me to review your quiz response:

- Indicate which answer(s) that you want me to review.
- Explain how you misunderstood the question or concept for each answer that was marked "wrong."
- Demonstrate your understanding of the concept being tested by explaining your answer to the question in two or three sentences.

This has been great for students who have test-taking anxiety or those who just don't do well with an assessment that measures their test-taking skills because it provides an alternate way for students to demonstrate their understanding of the concepts. This process also means I can keep the multiple-choice quiz format for students who want a quick way to demonstrate their understanding. These students do not have to write out their responses for every question. They can just choose to write out their responses for the questions that they missed.

I also like that the flexible quiz review process provides a more equitable assessment tool that does not create a lot of extra work for me. For each quiz, a few students choose to use the flexible quiz review process, but it is an optional process, and some students do not choose to use it or do not need it.

Here is a student response that talks about the flexible quiz review process in a student survey: "I think the quiz review was extremely helpful—it helped me learn how to review my mistakes and fully understand why it was the correct answer."

Of course, quizzes, rubrics, written feedback, and the capstone project are not the only assessments and assignments that can be designed to be multiple, flexible, equitable, and humanizing. Other teachers design their assignments and assessments to be student-centered and affirming of students' full selves in different ways. To show more of those multiple possibilities as well as the empowering effects of assignments and assessments designed for freedom, I am going to share another composite character counter-narrative. This story is about Ryan, a neurodivergent BIPOC middle school student with an IEP.

Ryan's Story

Ryan started middle school motivated to do his assignments and succeed in school, but it wasn't long before the cracks in the structure of his classes started to show. For example, despite having an accommodation to use a laptop in class, Ryan felt uncomfortable asking for this "special" accommodation because it marked him as different. It would have been great if his classes had allowed all students to use a laptop if needed, but that wasn't how his classes were designed.

Ryan also wasn't about to admit that what his teacher considered "a little bit of writing" was actually a *lot* for him. Since he was embarrassed to ask for his laptop accommodation, he decided that it would be easier if he just figured out his own accommodations. For example, on one science test, he was required to draw elliptical rings around planets, and the task was so tiring that he decided to make dots around the planet instead. This allowed him to complete the task and show his understanding of the concept. Ryan was pleased with this solution and was surprised when he was marked down for it.

In his English class, Ryan ran into even more rigidity. For example, the class was assigned vocabulary lists where the students were supposed to guess the meaning of vocabulary words from context clues and then look up the dictionary definition. The problem was that Ryan already knew the definitions of the vocabulary words and didn't see the point of doing vocabulary lists or other busy work. Eventually, he stopped doing work that he saw as pointless (literally, since they weren't graded) and chose to do only work that was graded.

Owing to incidents like this, it didn't take long for Ryan to become convinced that he was a bad student and test-taker. He didn't realize that his inability to do the assignments and assessments had nothing to do with internal deficits and everything to do with the inflexibility of assignment and assessment design.

Fortunately, in eighth grade, Ryan finally had teachers who designed his assignments and assessments to be multiple, flexible, equitable, and humanizing. One example was Mr. Jacobs, Ryan's Social Studies teacher. Mr. Jacobs gave students a choice wheel for assignments, allowing students to choose from anything from a board game to a podcast to a test to demonstrate their understanding of a concept. Ryan loved the multiplicity of options and started out with enthusiasm about creating a board game that showed how the intersectionality of gender, race, and class affected people's lives during the Industrial Revolution.

However, the project became so daunting that he began to lose focus and stamina. Eventually, he became frustrated and stopped working on the project. When Mr. Jacobs noticed Ryan's frustration, he said sympathetically, "Look, I've been seeing you work on the rules of your game, and it's obvious you understand these concepts inside and out. If the board game isn't working out for you, why don't you try another option to show what you know? Maybe a test."

Ryan couldn't believe that Mr. Jacobs had noticed how much he had learned through working on his game. He was relieved that Mr. Jacobs didn't lecture him about perseverance or work completion, but he didn't feel confident about his test-taking abilities, and he said so.

"I hear you," Mr. Jacobs said, "but I'm sure you can do this test. If anything gives you trouble, we'll just talk it out, and I'll give you credit that way."

Bolstered by Mr. Jacobs' encouragement and belief in his abilities, Ryan chose to take the test, and he ended up getting an A on it. The multiple options and flexibility Mr. Jacobs' built into the assignment helped Ryan gain agency in his learning, but just as important was the humanizing way Mr. Jacobs treated his students. This led Ryan to build confidence in his abilities as a student.

Another positive experience that built up Ryan's confidence took place in his science class. His teacher Ms. Joy noticed that Ryan wasn't doing the daily assignments in her class, so she took the time to ask him what might work better for him. Ryan was so used to teachers characterizing his behavior as "non-compliance" or "work refusal" that he was taken aback, but Ms. Joy seemed genuinely curious and non-judgmental in her question.

"I need time to think before starting an assignment," he mumbled. "I just hate having to do a million little assignments," he added, bracing himself for Ms. Joy to list all the reasons he should do these assignments.

Instead, she nodded thoughtfully. "That makes sense," she replied. "I think you would do better with larger project-based assignments. In fact, I'm realizing that quite a few students would benefit from project-based assignments. I'm going to need to add that option into the course."

A sense of relief filled him, and his whole body relaxed. "Yeah, that could work." He would have hated to be the only student doing a special project, but he wouldn't need to be embarrassed if it were an option for everyone.

And it *did* work. Once Ryan had the option to demonstrate his understanding of the course standards through projects instead of a "million little assignments," he could relax into his work instead of mustering up the energy and attention of constantly starting a new assignment.

Another class that helped Ryan grow, not only as a learner but as a whole person, was Ms. Day's English class. It was especially important for Ryan, a student of color, to have a teacher who was equity-minded and as culturally responsive and committed to culturally sustaining practices as Ms. Day. He liked how she was upfront about creating a classroom community that centered who students were, supporting students to accept one another and to allow each other to change and shift as they discussed race, sexual orientation, and friendships. She was clear that all her assignments were meant to support students as learners.

Ryan loved how all the assignments and activities in this class affirmed who he was. Activities like the community classroom circle where students could talk about what they wanted and book clubs that allowed students to read books that reflected their own identities or interests not only helped him gain a stronger sense of self, but also created a community of acceptance and support in the class.

Ryan also appreciated the portfolio assessment that let him choose what he wanted to include in the portfolio. As Ms. Day put it, the portfolios were meant to "help them tell their stories as learners." There were multiple assignments Ryan could include in his portfolio like a mask project that showed who they were on the inside and opened up to reveal who they were on the outside and writing reflections on community class circles or identity book clubs.

While Ryan actually liked doing these assignments, he wasn't comfortable about including work that was so personal as a reflection of his learning. However, he knew he could talk to Ms. Day about his concerns. Earlier in the year, Ms. Day had done an "empathy interview" where she had asked questions about how students learned. Her interview with Ryan felt less like an assessment and more like a conversation. He appreciated how his teacher actually wanted to understand how he was learning. Because of that experience, he felt comfortable bringing up his hesitation about the portfolio assignment with Ms. Day.

Not surprisingly, Ms. Day listened carefully and replied warmly, "Thank you for sharing your thoughts with me, Ryan. You know, the portfolio is flexible, so you don't have to include anything you don't want to. You can include anything that you're proud of or that you feel represents you or your learning."

Ryan knew that already, but it helped to hear this reminder. He felt light with relief that Ms. Day got where he was coming from.

"As a matter of fact," she added, "I was thinking about how excited you were about the environmental justice unit. Do you think you could focus your portfolio on the writing and reflections you did for that unit?"

Ryan remembered how much he enjoyed talking and writing about the book he read for the environmental justice book club. In fact, one reason he liked that book so much was that it had a BIPOC main character that Ryan could identify with. "Actually, that's perfect," he said.

It was important for Ryan to have the agency to choose what best represented his own interests and learning, and he was glad he discussed the portfolio with Ms. Day. Ryan felt seen and understood in Ms. Day's class, and that made him confident and empowered in his own learning.

As a result of his experience with these three teachers, Ryan was able to express his full authentic self, free from the restraints that had characterized his first two years of middle school. This is a freedom we can achieve for all our students and for ourselves— just by designing our classes and teaching with the principles of multiplicity, flexible design, equity, and humanizing pedagogy. That is the power of Anti-Oppressive UD.

Happily Ever After and a Greater Proportion of Hope

My own hope and Happily Ever After as a teacher comes from my students and their personal stories. However, I know that student success is often measured by data, so I decided to crunch some numbers to see what effect Anti-Oppressive UD curriculum and practices had on student grades. I compared two years (2016–2018) when I wasn't consciously using Anti-Oppressive UD principles in my classroom design with two years (2020–2022) when I started consciously using Anti-Oppressive UD principles.

I suspected there would be a difference, but I was surprised to find how *much* of a difference Anti-Oppressive UD made. The rate of students earning a 3.0 or better jumped from 47% to 80%.

To me, this is particularly impressive because the data from when I was using Anti-Oppressive UD was during the pandemic years—a time when student grades were generally plummeting. It's important to note that students did not achieve these results because I "inflated grades" or "lowered standards." I simply designed my curriculum, practices, policies, assignments, and assessments with the principles of multiplicity, flexible design, equity, and humanizing pedagogy.

My own success as a teacher is harder to quantify. It comes from the joy that fills me every time I walk into the classroom. That joy comes from the Anti-Oppressive UD framework that allows my students and me to create a world where we are all free to be ourselves. Yet I know there are hard times ahead for my students. As I write this final chapter, I am filled with a deep fear for the attacks that trans and BIPOC students will face—that all students with marginalized identities will face. Still, I am grateful to be a teacher in these times—to be able to hope and work with my students toward joy and freedom.

# Chapter 6 Teaching Toolkit Example

Here's an example of a capstone project assignment designed with principles of multiplicity, flexible design, equity, and humanizing pedagogy. This is the capstone assignment for a unit in an eleventh-grade English class. One pattern I have noticed in student surveys is that students often mention how clear structure and organization help make assignments accessible. Therefore, I'm modeling some concepts from the Universal Design for Learning (UDL) principle of multiple means of representation to break up my assignment into clear headers using a different font size or all caps, bullet-pointed lists, and multiple font styles like bold and italics to emphasize information. For example, I like putting due dates in bold so students can spot them easily. I'm also including the types of information that students have told me they find helpful. For the more detailed information like essay structure, I include the information in a link to a handout instead of cluttering the assignment with a lot of information.

REWRITING THE RULES CAPSTONE PROJECT ASSIGNMENT

Assignment Requirements

- Due dates (with a reminder of a flexible extension policy).
- Suggested page lengths.
- Information about headings and titles (even if you have no preference for headings or titles, it's helpful to say that so students don't have to wonder).
- Submission instructions (with a reminder that students can submit the assignment during the in-class workday).
- Font size and spacing. (I frame this as teacher accommodations. For example—"Please keep in mind that a standard font like Arial or Times New Roman of at least 12 point and double-spacing is an accommodation I am requesting.")

- Other elements necessary to the assignment like quotes from sources or citations. (For example, quotes from both the novel you chose to read for this unit and at least one of the articles and essays in this unit.)

Assignment Objective

The objective of the assignment is to create a capstone project that reflects your understanding of the unit concepts of "Rewriting the Rules."

Assignment Outcomes

- Understand the multiplicity and importance of diverse, intersectional representation.
- Demonstrate responsiveness to a multiplicity of cultures, identities, and histories.
- Express and sustain the student's own cultures, identities, and interests in ways that are meaningful to the student.
- Read closely to determine what the text says explicitly and to make logical inferences from it; cite specific textual evidence when writing or speaking to support conclusions drawn from the text. (CCSS for ELA 35)
- Write arguments to support claims in an analysis of substantive topics or texts, using valid reasoning and relevant and sufficient evidence. (CCSS for ELA 41)
- Draw evidence from literary or informational texts to support analysis, reflection, and research. (CCSS for ELA 41)

Assignment Overview

For the capstone project assignment, you will have the choice of writing either a literary analysis essay, an argument essay, a persuasive letter, or a short story/picture book/poem with a reflection essay.

Assignment Directions

All choices will be based on the novel you chose for the "Rewriting the Rules" unit and at least one article or essay in this unit. Please choose *one* of the following options to do for your capstone project:

1. Write a **literary analysis** on a theme of cultural identity in your novel. Please include supporting quotes from both your novel and at least one article or essay in this unit.
2. Write an **argument essay** for why your novel is important for diverse representation. Please include supporting quotes from both your novel and at least one article or essay in this unit.
3. Write a **persuasive letter** to the school board that argues for the importance of diverse representation in your novel and why it should not be banned. For this option, assume that the school board has banned your novel due to concerns about critical race theory, LGBTQ+ issues, or other issues that have been used to justify censorship of marginalized identities. Please include supporting quotes from both your novel and at least one article or essay in this unit.
4. Write a **short story, picture book, or poem** with diverse representation (this part of the project will *not* be evaluated) and a **reflection essay** (this part of the project *will* be evaluated). The reflection essay should reflect on how your novel and unit concepts helped shape your story, picture book, or poem. For this reflection paper, please include supporting quotes from both your novel and at least one article or essay in this unit.
5. If you have a **different idea** for your capstone project, please talk to me about it!

In addition, here are some other elements I typically include in an essay assignment.

Novel Choices and Articles/Essays in This Unit

Here, I would include a bulleted list of the novel choices and links to the articles and essays so students can find this information easily.

Directions for Teacher Feedback

Here, I would include the directions for student-centered feedback that I shared earlier in the chapter.

Hints and Handouts

Here, I would include a bulleted list of helpful hints (like using previous exercises and work for the essay) and links to documents on paper structure, writing a thesis, paragraph organization, rhetorical appeals, citations, sample outline, sample essay, and other instructional materials.

Teacher Accommodations

Here, I would include a bulleted list of accommodations I need, including a reminder for students to "Take ownership of their own voices" instead of using artificial intelligence (AI) generative programs as well as a reminder to request extensions before the original due date to make grading sustainable for me.

Grading Rubric

The last part I include is a grading rubric that I have designed with Anti-Oppressive UD principles. And speaking of that, here is the Teacher Toolkit Exercise!

Teacher Toolkit Exercise: Designing an Anti-Oppressive UD Grading Rubric

Now it's your turn to design an Anti-Oppressive UD grading rubric for one of your assignments! Here are some guiding questions to help you through your design process:

- Can your rubric be designed for *equity* by removing or replacing criteria that evaluate students on "norms," "conventions," and "correctness" that might be code for inequitable dominant-centric norms?
- Can your rubric be designed with non-evaluative categories that allow you to honor a *multiplicity* of voices and multiple ways of learning?
- Can your criteria be designed with open wording to allow for more *flexible* assessment?
- Can your criteria be designed to empower students in their voice, vision, and *humanity*?
- With the understanding that your rubric needs to be aligned with larger district or state standards, can you also include your own learning outcomes to design more *freedom* in your students' learning?

What This Tool Is For: You can use this tool to design an equitable assessment.

Works Cited

Baker-Bell, April. *Linguistic Justice: Black Language, Literacy, Identity, and Pedagogy.* Routledge, 2020.

"Common Core State Standards for English Language Arts and Literacy in History/Social Studies, Science, and Technical Studies." PDF. *Washington Office of Superintendent of Public Instruction*, 2011, ospi.k12.wa.us/student-success/resources-subject-area/english-language-arts/english-language-arts-learning-standards. Accessed 22 Oct. 2024.

Ma, Diana. "Equitable UDL Assessments" *Dianamaauthor.com*, 11 Nov. 2022, https://dianamaauthor.com/equitable-udl-writing-assessments/. Accessed 18 Nov. 2024.

For Product Safety Concerns and Information please contact our EU
representative GPSR@taylorandfrancis.com
Taylor & Francis Verlag GmbH, Kaufingerstraße 24, 80331 München, Germany

www.ingramcontent.com/pod-product-compliance
Lightning Source LLC
Chambersburg PA
CBHW070804230426
43665CB00017B/2483